Eucharist and American Culture

LITURGY, UNITY, AND INDIVIDUALISM

Dennis C. Smolarski, SJ

Paulist Press
New York/Mahwah, NJ

Imprimi Potest
Very Rev. John P. McGarry, SJ, Provincial
California Province, Society of Jesus
May 25, 2009

Unless otherwise noted, Scripture texts in this work are taken from the New Revised Standard Version: Catholic Edition Copyright © 1989 and 1993, by the Division of Christian Education of the National Council of the Churches of Christ in the United States of America. Used by permission. All rights reserved.

Excerpts from the English translation of the Order of Mass, and the General Instruction of the Roman Missal © 1971, 2002, International Committee on English in the Liturgy, Inc. All rights reserved. Used with permission.

Excerpts from *The Basic Sixteen Documents, Vatican Council II, Constitutions Decrees Declarations* (Inclusive Language Translation) Austin Flannery, OP (ed.), Northport, NY: Costello Publ. Co., 1996.

Cover and book design by Lynn Else

Library of Congress Cataloging-in-Publication Data

Smolarski, Dennis Chester, 1947–
    Eucharist and American culture : liturgy, unity, and individualism / Dennis C. Smolarski.
      p. cm.
    Includes bibliographical references.
    ISBN 978-0-8091-4670-3 (alk. paper)
    1. Church—Unity. I. Title.
    BV601.5.S66 2010
    262´.72—dc22

                                                                    2010000245

Published by Paulist Press
997 Macarthur Boulevard
Mahwah, New Jersey 07430

www.paulistpress.com

Printed and bound in the
United States of America

Contents

To the memory of all those who
have labored for unity
among Christians,
among nations,
among races.

Preface

The human race is daily faced with many challenges, among which are starvation and conflicts in Africa, political tensions in the Middle East, poverty, homelessness, AIDS, global warming, and the list goes on. Nevertheless, a special challenge that faces Christians in particular is the challenge to become *one* and to form the "body of Christ" in our world today.

This is the same challenge also faced by the early Christian church. For those of us who regularly walk into fast food restaurants in the twenty-first century and eat in the same room as people of different races, often speaking different languages, and of different economic classes, we readily accept the "self-evident" truth that "all men are created equal" (U.S. Declaration of Independence, par. 2). That reality has become part of the climate in most of the United States, and people accept that reality in most public places. However, Judea and Galilee and Corinth and Rome of 2000 years ago were quite different from New York or Chicago or Los Angeles today. Jews did not eat with Greeks, slaves did not eat with free men, lepers kept away from healthy people, and women were often separated from men. Social elites were expected to receive more and better food at certain meals, and where you sat at certain communal meals indicated your social rank.

So we may not immediately appreciate what a countercultural event the early Christian Eucharists were, with women and men, Jew and Greek, slave and free, the sick and the healthy, all united around the common Eucharistic table, and all eating of the same loaf and sharing in the same cup—they were truly *one in Christ* (see Gal 3:28).

Both in the early church and in our own time, every Eucharist challenges those whom God has gathered to remember who we are because of what we have become through our baptism into Christ's death and resurrection. At every Eucharist the gathered community celebrates who and what we are, the united body of Christ, in word and action. If Catholics could only become more aware of what we celebrate each time we gather for Mass, perhaps we can see the Eucharist as the source of life and energy to counteract the aspects of our culture that divide us. Perhaps then the Eucharist can truly unite us in the body of Christ—as countercultural as that may seem.

In a world marked by a multitude of differences and divisions—political, religious, racial, economic—wouldn't it be wonderful if the words of Jesus, "that they all may be one" (John 17:11), and repeated by Paul and others in various ways could be a reality! What if the divisions between Catholics and Protestants in Ireland became ancient history, along with the disagreements between Sunni and Shiite Muslims, or between Catholics and Orthodox Christians, or between Muslims and Jews, or between Americans of African and of European ancestry, or between Serbs and Croats? It would be very naïve to assume that such unity will occur tomorrow if it has eluded the grasp of humanity for the past several thousand years! Yet followers of Christ must keep Christ's hope and prayer for unity alive and do what they can to help that oneness become a reality.

This book is a reflection on Christ's prayer for unity and on how we foster that unity when we celebrate the Christian Eucharist and other liturgical celebrations. I examine some of the key moments during the celebration of the Mass that, according to official documents, attempt to foster unity and, additionally, refer to other aspects of liturgical celebrations that focus on the unity of the people of God. However, Christians do not celebrate the Eucharist or other sacraments in a vacuum. Each of us has been molded and influenced by our society and by the culture in which we live. Thus, I also refer to recent scholarly writings that address contemporary U.S. social phenomena, particularly a growing individualism and a lack of social connectedness, especially among the younger generations.

I hope the reflections I offer here will raise awareness, since I firmly believe that unless individuals are *aware* of what the problems are and of what the Lord desires of us all, then they can never take steps to address any such problems.

In addition, I do not intend this to be a book exclusively for liturgical professionals, such as priests, deacons, and parish directors of liturgy, who regularly serve God's holy people, although many times I do refer to official regulations. Neither do I intend this to be a work geared solely for academics, although I do refer to academic works published by scholars working in secular fields.

I do hope and pray that it will also be accessible to other lay women and men working in parishes, to young people eager to learn more about what Christians do (or are supposed to do) when they gather together for worship, and to all Christians who want to improve their personal relationships with others and understand more about what Jesus wanted his followers to do.

My sincere thanks to all who have read earlier drafts of this work and offered their thoughts, critiques, comments, and recommendations. In particular, let me acknowledge Deacon Ron Hansen; Prof. Eric Hanson; Mrs. Carolyn Mullally; Fr. J-Glenn Murray, SJ; Sr. Sharon McMillan, SND de N; Mrs. Kathleen Haas; Mr. Philip Flowers and those priests on sabbatical involved in the fall 2007 Vatican II Institute at Menlo Park, California. My special thanks to Mr. Nick Wagner, who offered valuable suggestions and helped with editing.

Once again, I would like to express my appreciation for the wonderful staff at Paulist Press for their assistance in seeing this project to completion.

CHAPTER 1

Introduction

John 17:21—"That they may all be one"

It was not uncommon, especially in the 1990s, to see people raise a banner at a football game with the numbers "3:16" displayed on it. You probably recognized that as a reference to the well-known verse from the Gospel of Saint John: "For God so loved the world that he gave his only Son, so that everyone who believes in him may not perish but may have eternal life" (John 3:16).

God's love is indeed a reality to be proclaimed and remembered. In addition, Christians need to proclaim God's initiative in sharing love by creating and interacting with the human race. We need to remember how God's love for us became visible through the gift of Jesus, who lived our life and died our death. John 3:16 also reminds us of God's intention that we share in eternal life through our faith in Christ.

LOVE ONE ANOTHER

Love is a theme repeated throughout the Christian Scriptures, especially in the Johannine writings. In John 15, Jesus reminds the disciples of his love for them and invites them to remain in love: "As the Father has loved me, so I have loved you; abide in my love" (John 15:9). He then gives them this instruction: "This is my commandment, that you love one another as I have loved you" (John 15:12). In the first letter of John, we read, "Beloved, since God

1

loved us so much, we also ought to love one another....God is love, and those who abide in love abide in God, and God abides in them" (1 John 4:11, 16).

Of course, few can forget Paul's great "hymn to love": "If I speak in the tongues of mortals and of angels, but do not have love, I am a noisy gong or a clanging cymbal....Love is patient; love is kind;..." (1 Cor 13:1–13). There is yet another Pauline hymn to love in the letter to the Romans, "Who will separate us from the love of Christ?...neither...height, nor depth,...will be able to separate us from the love of God in Christ Jesus our Lord" (Rom 8:35–39).

References to love abound in scripture, and we might indeed focus on love as the means for combating sin and its effects in the world. Love, however, is not the only theme in scripture, even if it is the best known. Another theme we might turn to in order to overcome the divisions caused by injustice, illness, and poverty is *unity*.

LOVE UNITES US

John's gospel includes the well-known "priestly prayer" of Jesus in chapter 17, depicting Jesus praying for his followers in the context of the Last Supper, immediately before going to the Garden of Gethsemane for his betrayal and arrest. In this "priestly prayer," we find the Lord explicitly praying several times for *unity* among his followers:

> that they may be one, as we are (John 17:11)...that they may all be one. As you, Father, are in me and I in you, may they also be [one] in us (John 17:21)...so that they may be one, as we are one (John 17:22)...that they may become completely one (John 17:23).

It is this simple prayer for unity by the Lord that is the leitmotif of this book. But these few words taken from John 17:21, "that they may all be one," and its variants, also need to be understood in the broader scriptural and first-century social context, to understand how striking they, in fact, are, and to understand how pervasive is this scriptural theme.

The Bible begins with an emphasis on unity. The one God brings order and unity out of chaos in the first chapter of Genesis. The original unity of human beings was destroyed when Cain killed Abel. Divisions then become more pronounced with the "confusion" of languages that God permitted because of human pride in building the Tower of Babel (Gen 11). In Christ, however, God reestablishes the original unity in all of creation. In his Letter to the Romans, Saint Paul emphasizes that it was through the *one* person Jesus Christ that *many* were saved, even though through *one* transgression *many* died (Rom 5:15–21).

The unity Jesus prayed for in John 17 is based on the oneness Jesus experienced with God the Father, expressed, for example, when Jesus said, "The Father and I are one" (John 10:30). Scripture also hints at Jesus' oneness with the Spirit and at unity within the Trinity when the newly-baptized Jesus is joined by the Father's voice and by the Spirit hovering as a dove (Luke 3:22); or when Jesus breathes on the apostles on Easter night to give them the gift of the Spirit (John 20:22), the Spirit that "remained" with him at his baptism (John 1:32-33).

Contemporary commentaries often overlook unity, however. Perhaps this is because unity makes more practical demands on us than the somewhat abstract ideal of *love*. Yet we should never forget that *love* and *unity* are interrelated. As Saint Thomas Aquinas argued, "love unites the beloved to the lover" (*Summ. Theol.*, Ia IIae, q 28, art 3). Since God is love (1 John 4:16), God must also be the source of unity as well.

John's Gospel expresses unity among Christ's followers in a variety of ways. For example, union with Christ and with others (through Christ) is the reality expressed in the biblical image of the vine and the branches (John 15:1–8). In this passage, the unity of the individual with Christ and with others is implicitly expressed in terms of the unity of a vine with its branches. Unity is also expressed by the image of the Good Shepherd (John 10) who tries to bring other sheep into his fold so that "there will be one flock, one shepherd" (John 10:16).

WE ARE ONE BODY IN CHRIST

Another biblical image for unity, used in the Pauline writings, is that of the one *body of Christ* (see 1 Cor 12:12–30 and elsewhere), in which individual Christians are seen as members of Christ's body, with Christ as the head (Eph 4:15–16). Although the image of the body in depicting unity is especially prominent in Paul's First Letter to the Corinthians, references to one body are also found in other letters of Paul. For example, Paul reminds the Romans, "We, who are many, are one body in Christ, and individually we are members one of another" (Rom 12:5), and he reminds the Colossians, "Let the peace of Christ rule in your hearts, to which indeed you were called in the one body" (Col 3:15).

There are other references to unity among Christians as well in Paul's writings. For example, in his Letter to the Galatians, Paul writes, "There is no longer Jew or Greek,…for all of you are one in Christ Jesus" (Gal 3:28). In his Letter to the Philippians, Paul seems to be pleading with them when he writes, "Make my joy complete: be of the same mind, having the same love, being in full accord and of one mind" (Phil 2:2). He then encourages them to avoid individualism when he continues, "Do nothing from selfish ambition or conceit, but in humility regard others as better than yourselves. Let each of you look not to your own interests, but to the interests of others" (Phil 2:3–4). Unity with God and among others is also implicit in other statements of Paul, for example, "it is no longer I who live, but it is Christ who lives in me" (Gal 2:20) and "God may be all in all" (1 Cor 15:28).

TOGETHER FOR A PURPOSE

The Gospels depict the Lord attempting, in numerous ways, through his actions, to unite different peoples, particularly individuals whom first-century Jews, for various reasons, normally spurned. For example, Christ straddled social boundaries when he interacted with women (as the Canaanite woman with the sick daughter [Matt 15] or the Samaritan woman at the well [John 4]), used non-Jews in teaching parables (the Good Samaritan [Luke 10]), and cured lepers (and it was the Samaritan leper who was the only one who gave thanks [Luke 17]!). Christ broke the boundary taboos repeatedly during his ministry, at meals, and in his teachings, by reaching out to those so often excluded in order to foster unity among people.

There are other indirect references to unity between individuals and Christ. For example, in Matthew 18:20, the Lord counsels his hearers that where two or three are gathered together in his name, he is there. The verb used here in Greek for "gathered together" is not the simple word for being "led (individually)" by another person to some location. Rather the text uses a verb with the prefix *syn-*, derived from the preposition *with*. Thus, the verb used indicates a communal action and is the root of the word *synagogue*, the place where people have been "gathered together" by God. When we "gather together" in Christ's name, it is not the same as being led by advertisements for sales at the local shopping mall, for example. In such a situation, many people go to the same physical location and are in one place together, but they are there as *individuals* rather than as a *community*. The biblical words indicate something more united, more communal. Similar Greek words with the *syn-* ("with") prefix are used elsewhere in the New Testament, as in Acts 10 in the context of eating and drinking.

In Matthew 25:31ff, Jesus narrates the parable about the last judgment and says, "Just as you did it to one of the least of these who are members of my family, you did to me." Here we read of a unity between an overlooked individual and the Lord himself. In Luke 16:19ff, we hear of the parable of the rich man and poor Lazarus who was overlooked, and who is reminiscent of those overlooked in Matthew 25 who imaged Christ to those who had eyes to see.

One could even suggest that the narration of the appearance of the risen Christ to the apostles on Easter night in John 20 was a call to community, since Thomas, who was not present, did not believe that Christ was raised because he had not been present with the others. Only when Thomas was present *with the others*, that is, in the community of the other apostles, on the following Sunday, was he able to experience the presence of the Risen Lord in a very vivid way. This scene suggests that experiencing the presence of the risen Christ, even today, demands that we join with others in community!

In Luke's gospel, there are three parables of the lost (Luke 15:1–32): the lost sheep, the lost coin, the lost son (i.e., the "prodigal son"). These can all be considered as stories of unity. They are parables of those who reestablish a lost unity: restoring the flock of ninety-nine to a united flock of one hundred, expanding the purse of nine coins back to ten, reuniting the lost son to the wholeness of family life.

Moreover, the Lord himself is a prime example of unity—one individual, with two natures, divine and human; one individual who unites all peoples together. He who, as God, is above all, by the power of the Holy Spirit became one with God's creation when he took flesh in the womb of the Virgin Mary, thereby uniting divinity and humanity. Paul sees Christ as uniting Jews and

Gentiles together in himself, "that he might create in himself one new humanity in place of the two, thus making peace" (Eph 2:15).

The Christian community is able to fulfill the prayer of Christ for unity, ultimately, by accepting the gift that is God's Spirit in their lives. At Confirmation, a Christian is signed with Chrism and told, "Be sealed with the Gift of the Holy Spirit." It is this Spirit of God, the Spirit of the Risen Christ, who, in turns, bestows other gifts among the community and draws Christians together into a deeper unity among themselves and with Christ.

UNITY IN DIVERSITY:
THE ULTIMATE CHALLENGE

Although the followers of Jesus are diverse in their numerous talents and God-given gifts, this diversity can be seen to be a sign of their one-ness since, as Paul writes, "all of these [gifts] are activated by one and the same Spirit" (1 Cor 12:11). It is the Spirit of the Risen Jesus, poured out on the Church, who draws Christians together into unity. That Spirit vividly reversed the divisions in the human race associated with the tower of Babel (Gen 11) when at Pentecost, the Spirit came as if by fire and wind among those in the upper room in Jerusalem, enabling the disciples to communicate with all present, whatever their origin (Acts 2:1-12). That gift of the presence of the Spirit prompted the early Christians to live in common and share all things in common (Acts 2:42-45).

Paul encouraged the Ephesians to preserve "the unity of the Spirit" (Eph 4:3). He then reminds the Ephesians that there is "one body and one Spirit" (Eph 4:4), just as there is "one Lord, one faith, one baptism; one God and Father of all, who is above all and through all and in all" (Eph 4:5-6). In a similar way, Paul wrote to the Philippians that they stand firm "in one spirit, striving side by side with one mind for the faith of the gospel" (Phil 1:27).

Throughout his ministry, Jesus tried to bring about a unity among individuals and in creation. He did this when he ate with sinners, spoke with Samaritans, cured lepers, preached about uniting the lost, and united divinity and humanity in his very person. It is little wonder, then, that the Last Supper, John's gospel records that the Lord prays that his followers, and indeed all humanity, may become one. It is also little wonder that unity among Christians, prompted by the Spirit, is a reoccurring image throughout the New Testament. It is, in fact, the ultimate challenge that faces Christians: to become one and to form the "body of Christ" in our world today.

In our quest to develop practical ways in which John 17:21 may become, in the twenty-first century, ever more a reality in our world, in our churches, in our homes, and in our hearts, let us first reflect on the theme of unity, particularly as related to the Eucharist, as mentioned in scripture and in the Christian tradition.

CHAPTER 2

Unity and the Eucharist

In a parable recounted in Luke's Gospel, Jesus commented on seating practices at wedding banquets and how someone who had taken a more prominent seat may be asked, to his embarrassment, to go to a lower one (Luke 14:7–11). In this context, one can understand the particular intensity of the complaints raised against Christ for his nontraditional manners at meals.

A commonly recorded complaint about Christ was that he ate with the wrong people, such as sinners and tax collectors (see, e.g., Matt 9:11, Mark 2:16, Luke 5:30, Luke 15:2). Although the story of Zacchaeus—who perched in a sycamore tree in Jericho—does not explicitly mention a meal (Luke 19), one would not stay at someone's house at the time of Christ and not be fed.

Even today, a foreigner travelling in the Middle East is usually offered something to drink upon entering a store catering to tourists, especially if the shopkeepers want to sell something! When Jesus announced that he would stay with Zacchaeus, people "grumbled" and said that Jesus was going "to be a guest of one who is a sinner" (Luke 19:7).

UNITY: THE PURPOSE OF THE TABLE

We seldom reflect on what Christ was trying to accomplish at meals. In most cases in the Gospels, whether describing a meal or a cure, the evangelist depicts the Lord as someone who makes use of the opportunity in order to teach and reveal a truth that some who were present may have overlooked. The healing of a blind beggar by Jesus (John 9) calls those who have their sight to reflect on how well, in fact, they "see" God's presence. The feeding of the 5,000 (Matt 14) invites those present to reflect on the nourishment from God that we all need. Speaking with a Samaritan woman (John 4) enables Jesus to teach her—and his disciples—that all people are worthy to receive God's word and the living waters that Jesus offers. When Jesus ate with those considered "sinners," he was bridging a social gap on earth that scripture hints will ultimately be erased by God in heaven. Isaiah describes the "feast of rich food" that God will provide on his holy mountain "for all peoples" (Isa 25:6). And in Luke, Jesus announces that "people will come from east and west, from north and south, and will eat in the kingdom of God" (Luke 13:29).[1] The inclusiveness mentioned in scripture is particularly striking in the context of social customs of the Middle East, where sharing a table meant sharing life.[2] It brought honor to a host to welcome someone special into the family home for a meal, and the wording of the Gospels indicates Jesus did, in fact, do this as a host (see Mark 2:15). In some cases, eating together could indicate a reconciliation, such as when King Jehoiachin was released from prison and allowed to eat at the table of the king of Babylon (Jer 52:31–34). Through his table fellowship with outcasts, Jesus was fulfilling the words spoken by the Lord through Ezekiel, "I will seek the lost, and I will bring back the strayed, and I will bind up the injured, and I will strengthen the weak" (Ezek 34:16). These actions of the Lord during meals contrast sharply with our modern society where eating on the run, alone, often at fast-food places, is considered normal! Through his table fellowship, Christ was bringing about the unity for which he prayed so intensely the night before he died.

The Pauline image of the Christian community forming *one body* in Christ is, as already noted, one image among many related to unity found in the New Testament. Although it is not the only image, because of its repeated use in scripture, it has a certain primacy. This image of *one body* reaches a high point, in a sense, in the communal partaking of the *one loaf and the one cup* at a celebration of the Eucharist, for Paul writes "because there is one bread, we who are many are one body, for we all partake of the one bread" (1 Cor 10:17). In his First Letter to the Corinthians, Paul criticizes the factions in that community, when he says, "When you come together as a church, I hear that there are divisions among you" (1 Cor 11:18–19). He suggests that because of these divisions, they lack true unity and thus are not really celebrating the Lord's Supper when they gather (1 Cor 11:20). He then reminds them that the Eucharistic bread and cup are not ordinary food but are, in fact, a sharing in the body and blood of Christ (1 Cor 11:23–28),[3] the body that was pierced and the blood that was shed on Calvary. Therefore they must always remember that "as often as you eat this bread and drink the cup, you proclaim the Lord's death until he comes" (1 Cor 11:26).

AN END TO DIVISION

Paul emphasizes to the Corinthians, "You are the body of Christ" (1 Cor 12:27) and bluntly states, "all who eat and drink without discerning the body, eat and drink judgment against themselves" (1 Cor 11:29). In effect, Paul was criticizing those who failed to recognize that the meal in which they participated was special and, thus ignored the practical implications that resulted from their participation. He was emphasizing the link between becoming Christ's body in the world and active participation in the eucharistic meal, and was taking to task those who desired union with Christ but did not accept the demands of union and interaction with fellow Christians. Paul, however, does not leave the Corinthians without any guidance. He suggests to them a way to form the body of Christ and eliminate the divisions in the community—the way of love—and his suggestions are contained in his great "hymn of love" (1 Cor 13) noted earlier.

The wonderful image of the Church as the "body of Christ" in the world today is one that has endured through the ages. In 1943, the late Pope Pius XII authored an encyclical on this image, *Mystici Corporis Christi* (The Mystical Body of Christ), and the Second Vatican Council referred to this same image in its documents. However, it seemed that this image often united people only on a spiritual level rather than leading Christians to a more tangible connectedness with others on a practical, day-to-day level. Hence, it is helpful to reflect on other images and references to unity. Even though the theme of unity is quite explicit in John's Gospel and in Paul's letters, some other images related to unity are overlooked, unfortunately, because of their subtlety. Often, these subtle references to unity occur within the context of meals.

For example, at the end of the parable of the Prodigal Son (Luke 15:11–32), the elder son expresses his disunity with his brother by refusing to come to the banquet table. Jesus uses the image of the wedding banquet given by a king for his son (Matt 22:1–14) as a sign of the Kingdom of Heaven and notes how some people may offer reasons why they are unable to come to the banquet, excluding themselves from union with others that is a common mark of such banquets. Near the end of the Book of Revelation, all the faithful are invited to come to the "marriage supper of the Lamb," an image of heavenly happiness (Rev 19:9).

In the accounts of the multiplication of the loaves and fish in the Gospels (Matt 14:13–21; Matt 15:23–38; Mark 6:32–44; Luke 9:10–17; John 6:1–13), the multitude are united by Jesus through eating from the same few loaves of bread and fish blessed by Jesus and distributed by the disciples.

In Acts 10:41, we read about those who ate and drank with the Lord after his resurrection. In this verse, the words for "ate" and "drank" are again communal verbs, with the Greek prefix *syn-*, which means *with*. As already noted, the nuance this prefix gives is that such meals were *communal* experiences of "co-eating" and "co-drinking" with other people and with the Risen Lord.

With this background, we can understand how the early Christian Eucharists challenged the social norms of the day. To have people of different genders, nationalities, and social statuses all dining together was a radical challenge to the organization of society (see, e.g., Gal 3:28). Social status no longer made any difference when someone was present at the Lord's Supper. Some of these early Christians, who might be considered "upper class" in contemporary terms, seem to have accepted in their lives the same humility that Christ did when he humbled himself and became one with the human race. As Paul writes so eloquently in Philippians 2, Christ, "though he was in the form of God, did not regard equality with God as something to be exploited, but emptied himself, taking the form of a slave, being born in human likeness. And...he humbled himself" (Phil 2:6–8).[4]

UNITY IN THE EARLY CHURCH

In addition to being an ongoing theme in the Christian Scriptures, unity, and particularly the link between unity and the Eucharist, was a topic of concern of the early Church. In fact, it has been an ongoing concern of Christians throughout the ages. The image of the "body of Christ" was used quite often in post-biblical writings. For example, the *Didache*, a late-first-century Christian document, uses the image of the one Eucharistic loaf to symbolize the unity of the Church gathered in prayer. One ancient prayer included begins with the words:

> As this broken bread was once scattered upon the mountains and being gathered together became one, so

> may your Church be gathered together from the ends
> of the earth into your kingdom. (9:4)

Saint Clement of Rome (died c. 100), in his *Letter to the Corinthians*, admonishes them, "Why do we tear apart and divide the body of Christ? Why do we revolt against our own body?" (Clem. Cor. 46:7; used in the *Liturgy of the Hours*, Office of Readings, Monday of the Fourteenth Week in Ordinary Time).

Saint Ignatius of Antioch (died c. 110), in his *Letter to the Ephesians*, uses a musical image in addressing unity when he writes:

> Every one of you should form a choir, so that, in har-
> mony of sound through harmony of hearts, and in
> unity taking the note from God, you may sing with one
> voice through Jesus Christ to the Father....It is then an
> advantage to you to live in perfect unity,... (Ig. Eph. 4:2;
> used the in *Liturgy of the Hours*, Office of Readings,
> Second Sunday in Ordinary Time)

In his *Letter to the Magnesians*, Ignatius writes:

> when you meet together there must be one petition,
> one prayer, one mind, one hope in love and in holy joy,
> for Jesus Christ is one and perfect before all else. You
> must all be quick to come together, as to one temple of
> God, one altar, to the one Jesus Christ, who came forth
> from the one Father, while still remaining one with
> him, and returned to him. (Ig. Magn., 7:1–2; used in the
> *Liturgy of the Hours*, Office of Readings, Monday of
> Sixteenth Week in Ordinary Time)

Over a century later, Saint Cyprian (died 258), in his *Treatise on the Lord's Prayer* (no. 8), wrote that Christ, who preaches peace and unity did not want us to pray by ourselves in private or for ourselves alone. We do not say "My Father, who art in heaven," ... Rather, we pray in public as a community, and not for one individual but for all. For the people of God are all one. (Used in the *Liturgy of the Hours*, Office of Readings, Monday of the Eleventh Week in Ordinary Time)

In Saint Gregory of Nyssa's (died c. 385) *Homily on the Song of Songs* (Hom. 15; used in *Liturgy of the Hours*, Office of Readings, Seventh Sunday of Easter), we read:

When love has entirely cast out fear, and fear has been transformed into love, then the unity brought us by our Savior will be fully realized, for all [people] will be united with one another through their union with the one supreme Good.

Saint Cyril of Alexandria (died c. 445), in his commentary on the *Letter to the Romans*, writes, "Though many, we are one body, and members of one another, united by Christ in the bonds of love" (Cpt 17:7; used in the *Liturgy of the Hours*, Office of Readings, Saturday, Fourth Week of Easter).

MORE RECENT UNITY THEMES

Centuries later, Saint Thomas Aquinas (died 1274), in his *Summa Theologica*, linked the Eucharist with unity when he wrote, "the reality of this sacrament [*res sacramenti*] is the unity of the Mystical Body" (*SummTheol*, IIIa, q 73, art 3; also see IIIa, q 73, art 2). More recently, the theme of unity was also mentioned at the Second Vatican Council, for example, in the Dogmatic Constitution on the Church, *Lumen Gentium*. In this decree we read, that God has, however, willed to make women and men holy and to save them, not as individuals without any bond between them, but rather to make them into a people who might acknowledge him and serve him in holiness (no. 9)...strengthened by the body of Christ in the Eucharistic communion, [the faithful] manifest in a concrete way that unity of the people of God which this most holy sacrament aptly signifies and admirably realizes. (no. 11)

In some of his writings, Pope John Paul II also addressed the theme of community and unity as well. For example, in his 2003 encyclical, *Ecclesia de Eucharistia* (On the Eucharist and the Church), the late pope wrote, "Eucharistic communion also confirms the Church in her unity as the body of Christ" (no. 23). Later in the same encyclical he wrote, "Our longing for the goal of unity prompts us to turn to the Eucharist, which is the supreme sacrament of the unity of the People of God, in as much as it is the apt expression and the unsurpassable source of that unity" (no. 43, also see nos. 21, 24, 42).

In his 2005 encyclical on love, *Deus Caritas Est* (God is love), Pope Benedict XVI links personal union with Christ with union with other Christians and with the Eucharist. He writes:

Union with Christ is also union with all those to whom he gives himself. I cannot possess Christ just for myself; I can belong to him only in union with all those who have become, or will become, his own. Communion draws me out of myself toward him, and thus also towards unity with all Christians. We become "one body," completely joined in a single existence. Love of God and love of neighbor are now truly united: God incarnate draws us all to himself. (no. 14)

Two years later, in his 2007 encyclical on hope, *Spe Salvi*, Pope Benedict XVI again raises the topic of unity and community when he says:

> This real life, towards which we try to reach out again and again, is linked to a lived union with a "people," and for each individual it can only be attained within this "we." It presupposes that we escape from the prison of our "I," because only in the openness of this universal subject does our gaze open out to the source of joy, to love itself—to God. (no. 14)

The theme of unity among Christians is found not only in scripture, patristic writing, academic treatises, and formal magisterial statements of councils and popes, but also in the day to day *lex orandi*, ("norm of prayer," i.e., liturgical texts) that the Church uses in celebrating the Eucharist. Although the words may pass us by because we have become so accustomed to them, at almost every Mass, the most commonly used Eucharistic prayers include explicit prayers for unity.

In Eucharistic Prayer II, we hear, "May all of us who share in the body and blood of Christ be brought together in unity by the Holy Spirit." Eucharistic Prayer III includes the words, "Grant that we, who are nourished by his body and blood, may be filled with his Holy Spirit, and become one body, one spirit in Christ." In Eucharistic Prayer IV, the text reads, "Gather all who share this one bread and one cup into the one body of Christ, a living sacrifice of praise." In Eucharistic Prayer I for Reconciliation, we pray, "By the power of your Holy Spirit make them one body, healed of all division."[5]

Such words referring to unity, and others that are not quite as explicit, all remind us that what we celebrate at the Eucharist is not merely the presence of Christ in the eucharistic bread and wine.

We celebrate the unity that Christ's presence should form in our world when those assembled realize that Christ is present among them when they truly form the Body of Christ.

FUNDAMENTAL QUESTIONS

The long litany of statements related to unity throughout the 2,000 years of Christian history invite us ask some questions fundamental to our lives as Christians. For example, what is my experience of *unity*—in my family, at work, in my neighborhood, in my parish, as a resident of the United States, as a member of Christ's Church? Pope Benedict XVI hints that some Christians today may live in a "prison of our 'I'," although they may not realize it. How do we escape from that prison? All of need to ponder the meaning of the pope's words, "I cannot possess Christ just for myself."

But how do we make sure that the pervasive influences in our contemporary society do not overwhelm the gentle voices of our faith tradition leading us *together* to a deeper unity with our God and with one another?

The rest of this book will try to raise questions, directly and indirectly, about the contemporary American culture and about our ideal celebration of the Eucharist. In chapter 3, we will look at recent research that has focused on the phenomenon of the decreasing numbers of people involved in social groups and activities. Then in chapter 4, we will consider the nature of *worship*, fundamentally a communal activity, and how this, in fact, contrasts with *prayer*, fundamentally an individual activity, and how both are needed for a balanced spiritual life. Following that, in chapters 5, 6, and 7, we will look at the liturgical documents, especially the *General Instruction of the Roman Missal* (GIRM), and see what kind of vision those documents present about the unity of those assembled and its relationship to posture, song, the use of "one bread and one cup," architectural issues, and other aspects of eucharistic and other liturgical celebrations. Chapters 8 and 9 offer some thoughts about how a united "Body of Christ" can be an agent of transformation in the world, and about the ongoing challenge posed by significant aspects of American and contemporary technological culture becoming pervasive throughout the world, often overwhelming the best of older local traditions that fostered social unity. The book concludes with a few discussion questions that could be used by groups eager to reflect on the issues raised.

Chapter 3

Opportunities and Challenges

The ideal of *unity*, the ongoing refrain in scripture and in Christian writings throughout the ages, is not something with which contemporary American Catholics easily resonate. Even those who regularly attend Mass seem to be more influenced by the culture in which they live than the scripture they hear and the unifying symbols and actions that are part of every liturgy.

What many of have forgotten (or never learned) is that when we celebrate Eucharist, we are recalling and even actualizing our unity as one body in Christ. We need to recover a deeper and more widespread understanding that our celebration of the paschal mystery makes us one in that mystery. Then, like the early church, our worship will counteract the effects of individualism and make us a beacon of hope for the eventual unity of the world.

MOVING TOWARD A
MORE UNIFIED WORLD

Nevertheless, if the unity that Christ prayed for does not exist within our Christian communities, how can we ever hope that Christians can be a leaven in our world for that same unity? And perhaps that is where there may be a significant yet subtle challenge for Christians—the challenge of understanding contemporary cultural forces that militate against Christ's prayer for unity.

One must start somewhere in responding to such opportunities and challenges. Of course, the first place to start is usually with oneself! (Remember that "Charity begins at home!" and so should most other endeavors.) Without realizing that each of us is part of a larger Christian community and that, individually, we need to reach out to others in that community of faith, we can never hope that unity in our Church or world will become more of a reality. When someone realizes the importance of fostering unity, then one can share one's hopes and dreams with acquaintances and friends starting with one's parish or faith community. The desire to build unity should usually precede the more practical lists of things to do (which can vary from parish to parish), and some suggestions will be offered later in this book about ways to foster and build up unity.

The unity that Jesus prayed for is a unity based on a union with God who is love (see Matt 22:37, "You shall love the Lord your God…"). It is a unity that links one person with another in mutual love and respect (see Matt 22:38, "You shall love your neighbor…"). As already noted, it is unity that fosters both community and a communal life reflective of the life of the early Church, where the early Christians "devoted themselves to the apostles' teaching and fellowship…" (Acts 2:42) and "all who believed were together and had all things in common" (Acts 2:44).

Unfortunately, U.S. culture does not foster this sort of unity, which is often characterized by the term "rugged individualism." In contrast to the biblical ideal, the unity fostered by typical American values is one that seems to encourage everyone to wear the same style of Levis, or to have the same iPods, or to buy the same cell phones, or to give everyone else the "space" to do his or her own thing without any commitment to any sort of broader societal behavioral norms.

To reflect more fruitfully on Christ's prayer for unity, let us consider the context in which Americans now find themselves. In his book, *The Spiritual Exercises*, Saint Ignatius Loyola recommends beginning a period of prayer with a "composition of place" and sometimes a "composition of history" (e.g., *Spiritual Exercises*, nos. 47, 65, 91, 103). It will help us to understand the American context if we similarly begin with "compositions of place and history." We need to reflect, albeit briefly, on how people interacted in the past, as well as reflect on the current situation, and then look at how, ideally, liturgical celebrations should reflect the scriptural values mentioned earlier, rather than the cultural "values" that influence us now.

FOUNDATIONAL VALUES

Almost four centuries ago, John Donne (1573–1631) wrote:

> No man is an island, entire of itself; every man is a piece of the continent, a part of the main....Any man's death diminishes me, because I am involved in mankind.... (Meditation 17, *Devotions upon Emergent Occasions*, written 1624).

In a sense, Donne recast thoughts expressed almost 1,700 years earlier by Marcus Tullius Cicero (106–43 BCE). In *De Officiis*, Cicero wrote:

> We are not born for ourselves alone....We are born for the sake of other human beings...that they may be able mutually to help one another...thus by our skill, our industry, and our talents to cement human society more closely together. (Bk 1, par. 22)

A few paragraphs later Cicero speaks about injustice and refers to "another kind of injustice," where individuals do not do things they could. He labels such people as "traitors to social life," who "contribute to it none of their interest, none of their effort, none of their means" (Bk 1, par. 29). Unfortunately, such sentiments of unity and connectedness expressed centuries earlier may seem quaint and hopelessly outdated to many Americans today.

"Individualism" is not a new phenomenon in American life. In the 1830s, a French lawyer, Alexis de Tocqueville, travelled extensively in the United States to report on the American prison system. As a result of his travels, Tocqueville not only published a report on the prison system, but also a multivolume work on politics in the United States, entitled *De la démocratie en Amérique*.[1] This was one of the first sociological studies of American life and, in his work, Tocqueville was one of the first to use the term "individualism" to describe one of the characteristics (what he sometimes called "habits of the heart") of American life.

In his writings, Tocqueville was careful to distinguish "individualism" from "egotism" (which, for Tocqueville was an "exaggerated love of self"). Tocqueville used "individualism" to describe the reality of individuals who have isolated themselves from others and withdrawn into a close circle of family and friends.[2] For Tocqueville, "individualism" is regrettable, yet an unavoidable by-product of America's "self-evident" truth that all are created equal[3] and have an equal stance in law. While critical of "individualism" in U.S. society in the early nineteenth century, Tocqueville saw hope in the reality that Americans were "forever forming associations."[4] Tocqueville mentions various kinds of such voluntary associations—commercial, industrial, religious, moral—and seemed to see these associations as a way to balance the negative aspects of "individualism." For Tocqueville, as long as Americans were eager to form and join "associations," especially those with a civil orientation, civic life would be healthy.[5]

In 1985, American sociologist and Berkeley professor Robert N. Bellah and colleagues published, *Habits of the Heart: Individualism and Commitment in American Life*,[6] which addresses various issues related to private life and public life in the United

States. Chapter Six of Bellah's book, in particular, focuses on "Individualism." There Bellah notes, "Individualism lies at the very core of American culture" (p. 142), but also cautions, "some of our deepest problems both as individuals and as a society are also closely linked to our individualism" (p. 142).

Bellah also notes that Americans experience ambivalence about their individualism. He writes:

> What this suggests is that there is a profound ambivalence about individualism in America among its most articulate defenders. This ambivalence shows up particularly clearly at the level of myth in our literature and our popular culture. There we find the fear that society may overwhelm the individual and destroy any chance of autonomy unless he stands against it, but also recognition that it is only in relation to society that the individual can fulfill himself and that if the break with society is too radical, life has no meaning at all. (p. 144)

The fact that "individualism" has been a part of U.S. culture for so long makes Christ's desire for unity truly countercultural in the current climate.[7]

In the early 1800s, when Tocqueville visited the United States, he perceived a delicate balance between the individualism based on political equality and what then seemed to be the constant desire of people to "form associations." In many ways, that older cultural climate of the United States permitted great tolerance toward immigrants and encouraged entrepreneurship and creativity, as examples. Today, however, people are less eager to "form associations," and thus there are fewer social antidotes to some of the negative aspects of individualism. As a result, there are subtle and not-so-subtle tendencies in the U.S. culture that clash with authentic religious traditions that lead believers toward unity and community. It has been only with much difficulty that laws have been passed recently in various states restricting an individual's "right" to smoke in certain public places or to drink a certain amount of alcohol and then drive. When society favors personal sovereignty over benefits to society, there are numerous ramifications in family interactions and religious organizations. When given a choice between "what I feel like doing" and "what is beneficial or helpful for the group to which I belong," within the contemporary U.S. culture, what benefits the individual is often chosen over what may benefit the group. For example, many families know the tension that occurs when the desires of an individual (whether adult or child) seem to overwhelm the tranquility of the family unit. And how often have parents had to deal with a child who didn't want to go to church or orchestra practice or sports practice because the child valued his or her personal desire over membership in the group. All these examples (and other similar scenarios) point to the various cultural forces that are real and affect our lives.

OBSTACLES TO UNITY

Because of these forces, Catholics who live in the United States need to discover what cultural obstacles exist that negatively influence the way they live out their lives as Catholics and particularly how they affect the ways Catholics participate in worship.[8] Some of these cultural tendencies and obstacles are, in fact, visible in the area of liturgy and communal worship.[9] In a 2004 article, Martin Connell suggested that Americans, in general, have an aversion to ritual.[10] He then notes the individualist threads pertaining to religion that are common in the writings of various significant U.S. authors. For example, Connell notes that Emily Dickinson wrote, "I keep [the Sabbath] staying at Home" and Ralph Waldo Emerson wrote, "We must go [to church] alone."

In addition to Bellah and Connell, various other scholars have also published a wide range of material on the deterioration of a communal spirit, the rise of individualism, and the "epidemic of loneliness," the last term referring to the significant rise in individuals seeking medical treatment for feeling alone, depressed, or isolated.[11]

It does seem strange that fewer people become involved in communal activities while at the same time a greater number of individuals complain that they are feeling more and more lonely. If individuals who experience loneliness also regularly attend liturgical celebrations, which should foster community among those assembled, one can rightly wonder about the success of such celebrations in achieving the Lord's wishes.

Loneliness is related to depression, as various psychological studies have pointed out, and the incidence of depression is often related to age cohorts. Harvard professor Robert D. Putnam, in his 2000 book *Bowling Alone*,[12] has pointed out:

> Public health epidemiologists using a variety of different methodologies have confirmed a long-term trend toward increasing depression and suicide that is generationally based. Depression has struck earlier and much more pervasively in each successive generation, beginning with the cohorts born after 1940. For example, one study reported that "of those American born before 1955, only 1 percent has suffered a major depression by age 75; of those born after 1955, 6 percent has become depressed by *age 24*." Psychologist Martin Seligman concludes that "the rate of depression over the last two generations has increased roughly tenfold...."
>
> ...Between 1950 and 1995 the suicide rate among adolescents aged fifteen to nineteen more than quadru-

pled, while the rate among young adults aged twenty to twenty-four, beginning at a high level, nearly tripled...this explosive growth in youthful suicide coincided with an equally remarkable decline in suicide among older groups. (p. 261)

INDIVIDUALISM, DEPRESSION, AND A DECLINE IN "SOCIAL CAPITAL"

Thus, the increase in depression and suicide among younger cohort groups is related to a greater sense of individualism and a deterioration of a sense of community. It is significant that a country such as Greece, with a strong family culture and significant rural atmosphere in the many islands, has only about a quarter of the number of suicides (about 3.2 percent) in comparison with the United States (about 11.0 percent).

In 1988, Princeton professor Robert Wuthnow published *The Restructuring of American Religions*, a sociological study on religion in America since World War II.[13] He describes the initial vision of religious faith and practices in terms of community, but also notes the growth of religious individualism. He writes:

The vision of faith was only partially discoverable by individuals; it required the support and inspiration of a community of believers. Religious practice was prototypically conceived in Western, Judeo-Christian terms as a commitment to a public body, not a life of mystical isolation. (p. 55)

Later he states,

The emphasis on individual piety was consistent with broader individualistic orientations in American cul-

ture....Less obvious at the time was the fact that religious individualism was a mode of cultural adaptation
that would greatly influence the character of American
religion in the coming decades. (p. 57)

From his academic discipline of political science, Putnam
also provides an analysis of the contemporary phenomenon of
fewer people being involved in social activities, building up what is
often termed "social capital."[14] There was a time when most
people bought into the reciprocity model perhaps best expressed
by Yogi Berra, "If you don't go to somebody's funeral, they won't
come to yours."[15] Peak involvement in many such social and communal activities occurred in the late 1950s and early 1960s. Since
that time there has been a steady and, in some cases, a precipitous
decline.[16]

As examples, Putnam notes the following (generally speaking about the changes between the early 1960s and the late 1990s):

daily newspaper readership among people under thirty-five
dropped from two-thirds in 1965 to one-third in 1990 (p.
36) (this was even before internet become commonplace
in homes!)

voting in the United States is down by about a quarter over
the last 20–30 years (p. 37)

the number of people seeking public office decreased by 15
percent (p. 42)

the number of PTA members decreased by a half a million
members between 1990 and 1997 (although public school
enrollment grew by over 5 million) (p. 56)

church attendance fell about 20 percent (p. 59)

the percentage of people attending club meetings in 1975 at
least once a year was 64 percent, whereas in 1999 the number had fallen to 38 percent (p. 61)

10 percent fewer people claim church membership and involvement in religious activities has fallen by 25–50 percent (p. 72)

among Catholics, the Catholic percentage of the population grew about 1–1.5 percent per decade but Mass attendance has steadily decreased[17] (pp. 75–76)

union membership decreased from 32.5 percent in 1955 to 14.1 percent in 1997 (pp. 81–82)

families eating dinner together declined from 50 percent to 34 percent (pp. 100–101)[18]

the number of people bowling as members of leagues has steadily declined since the early 1980s so that there may not be any significant membership in bowling leagues at the end of the first decade of the twenty-first century (pp. 112–13)

driving alone increased 30 percent (p. 212).

What is also striking from the data is that the decline is greater among those with greater education. For example, the decline in attendance at public meetings among college-educated decreased from 34 percent to 18 percent (p. 46). In addition, the data show that participation remains constant among age cohort groups. Thus, we see that people in the same age cohort who were active 30 years ago are still active now, but the younger cohort groups, as a whole, are less involved (p. 62, also see p. 141 for generational differences in trust of others, and p. 219 for generational differences in reading newspapers).

Another scholar, Jean M. Twenge, is on the faculty of San Diego State University and writes from her discipline of psychology. In her 2006 book, *Generation Me*,[19] Twenge describes many of the characteristics of the post-"baby boomers" generation. Twenge labels these young adults as "Generation Me," reflecting both that they are the "Millennial Edition" generation and that they are usually more concerned about "me" than about anyone else. As Twenge points out, this generation is noted for its sense of individualism[20] and entitlement. She points out that a 2005 Associated Press article labeled the current generation of young people as "The Entitlement Generation" (p. 214). Twenge also notes, "Boomers may have thought they invented individualism, but like any inventor, they were followed by those who truly perfected the art" (p. 48). Several times Twenge links this individualism to the decline in membership in social groups described by Putnam (see pp. 35, 110) and linked to generational shifts (see pp. 35, 141). For example, she repeats Putnam's findings about voter participation by noting that in 1972, participation by 18- to 20-year-olds was 48 percent, but in 2000, it had dropped to 28 percent (p. 143). Twenge's findings reflect earlier concerns about younger individuals in the workforce. For example, Labor economist Peter Pestillo in 1979 wrote, "The young worker thinks primarily of himself. We are experiencing the cult of the individual, and labor is taking a beating preaching the comfort of coalition."[21] Twenge notes that a study of news stories published (or aired) during the two decades between 1980 and 1999 found a large increase in self-reference words (e.g., I, me, mine) and a marked decrease in collective words (e.g., humanity, country) (p. 51).[22]

In 2009, Twenge, in collaboration with W. Keith Campbell, of the Department of Psychology at the University of Georgia, published *The Narcissism Epidemic: Living in the Age of Entitlement*. In this book, the authors examine what can be considered to be one of the by-products of an exaggerated individualism, namely the increase in narcissistic personality traits, especially among younger Americans.[23] Although labeling narcissism as an "epidemic" in the United States, they point out that other cultures are still somewhat immune from the almost obsessive focus on the self to the exclusion of others.[24]

INDIVIDUALISM AND RELIGION

In addressing religious issues, in *Generation Me*, Twenge quotes Jeffrey Arnett's 2004 book, *Emerging Adulthood*,[25] in noting that the belief systems of young people are "highly individualized" (Twenge, *Generation Me*, p. 34). This is the same point made by Putnam as well, namely that individuals have shifted to "privatized religion" with less communal involvement and support (Putnam, *Bowling Alone*, pp. 73–74). Others have pointed out that young adults often describe themselves as "spiritual" rather than as "religious" since "spiritual" often indicates a longing for the transcendent in a individualistic way, rather than "religious" which is linked to social groups, ritual practices, and organized religions.[26] Instead of following the biblical injunction to "outdo one another in showing honor" (Rom 12:10), in other words, to put the other person first, members of Generation Me often give the impression that they are oblivious that anyone else is alive (except possibly a close group of friends).

Twenge also points to the companion phenomenon of loneliness. As she notes, "It's almost as if we are starving for affection…we're malnourished from eating a junk-food diet of instant messages, e-mail, and phone calls, rather than the healthy food of live, in-person interaction" (p. 110). "But Generation Me often lacks other basic human requirements: stable close relationships, a sense of community….Our grandparents may have done without television…, but they were usually not lonely…" (p. 136).[27] It is a pity that more young people have not taken to heart the words of the founder of the Catholic Worker movement, Dorothy Day, with which she concludes her autobiography, *The Long Loneliness*, "We have all known the long loneliness and we have learned that the only solution is love and that love comes with community. It all happened while we sat there talking, and it is still going on."[28]

In 2007, Professor Wuthnow published a new study, *After the Baby Boomers*, specifically examining the religious practices of contemporary 20- and 30-year-old young adults. In it, he addresses issues raised by Putnam and others, such as of individualism, community, and social capital, and offers an analysis of the religious behavior of young adults associated with various religious groups, including Catholics in general and Hispanic Catholics as a subgroup.[29]

Others have connected the rise in the individualistic mentality to other American societal problems. For example, in a 2003 Op-Ed column entitled, "The Power of Marriage," *New York Times* columnist David Brooks writes:

> Today marriage is in crisis....Marriage is in crisis because marriage, which relies on a culture of fidelity, is now asked to survive in a culture of contingency. Today, *individual choice is held up as the highest value*: choice of lifestyles,...of identities,...of cell phone rate plans. Freedom is a wonderful thing, but the culture of contingency means that the marriage bond, which is supposed to be a sacred vow til death do us part, is now more likely to be seen as an easily cancelled contract.[30] (italics added)

A humorous, but no less serious examination of contemporary funeral customs is found in a 2006 *New York Times* column by John Leland entitled, "It's My Funeral and I'll Serve Ice Cream if I Want To"[31] (note three self-referent words in the title). The article describes the nontraditional "services" that people are planning for their own funerals, wanting them to have a "personal" touch, and seemingly without regard for any sort of social expectations. Also lacking in such contemporary "celebrations of life" is the ritual that enables the community of the living to mourn well as a group.[32]

In an era when most Americans have increased electronic means of communications—radio, television, wired phones, cell phones, computers—we have, at the same time, the new phenomenon that more and more people stay in "contact" (derived from the root Latin words *cum* = "with" and *tactus* = "touch," and thus meaning *common-touch* or *mutual-touch*) without actually physically touching another. Instead of fostering common activities, such new electronic tools for communication seem to be deepening individualism and isolationism.[33] We have probably all been in situations where cell phone users seem to be oblivious to how annoying they are to those nearby,[34] to say nothing of the drivers in cars or pick-up trucks with open windows, showing their cutting-edge stereo systems to an entire neighborhood with more decibels than a jet plane taking off!

The American way of "(non)-socializing" may seem odd to people of other cultures. A few years ago, a seminarian related an anecdote to me about an incident that occurred in the early 2000s when he was visiting another country with several other younger seminarians. He and his hosts found it odd that some of the other seminarians saw nothing unusual about jogging in the evening around the same time that others were having the evening meal. The seminarian who was narrating the incident tried to explain his confreres' behavior by referring to how important exercise was for many younger Americans and that some of the joggers were concerned about their health and weight. Nevertheless, such individualistic behavior at mealtime, a privileged time of socialization in many cultures, is often construed as a major social faux pas in non-American cultural settings.

Yet, we must acknowledge that the cultural makeup of the U.S. population is far from static and has never been homogeneous. In almost every large metropolitan area there have, for decades, been ethnic neighborhoods, such as San Francisco's famous Chinatown, Chicago's Polish districts, or Brooklyn's Italian neighborhoods. More recently, Vietnamese, Korean, Latino, or Indian people are establishing neighborhoods in some metropolitan areas because of recent immigrations. The recent influx of various cultural groups also has implications for church membership and attendance.

Just as secular social practices have changed over the last half century, there has also been a change in the dynamics of Church membership as well. In 2008, the Pew Forum on Religion and the Public Life published their "U.S. Religious Landscape Survey 2008," summarizing the results of their survey.[35] In it, we find detailed information about the religious composition of the United States and an analysis of the changes in religious affiliation by Americans.

The Pew Forum Survey notes that the percentage of the adult U.S. population who identify themselves as Catholics remains fairly constant over the years, at around 25 percent (p. 7), but that a larger percentage (31 percent) note that they had been raised as Catholics (pp. 6, 23). Overall, the Pew Survey suggests that slightly over 10 percent of adults have left the Catholic Church (pp. 7, 25), but that the overall percentage of Catholics remains constant because of new immigrants and some converts.

Some of the conclusions may be subject to debate. For example, the Center for Applied Research in the Apostolate (CARA) at Georgetown University raises questions about whether the Catholic population and the retention rate were underestimated.[36] But whatever the exact percentage is, one cannot deny the reality that religions, Catholicism included, are also losing members, sometimes in significant numbers. In various ways, this loss of membership in faith communities mirrors the loss of membership in other social organizations.

UNITY IS COUNTERCULTURAL

Unfortunately, the lessons of the Gospels and the themes of unity mentioned elsewhere in Christian scriptures may make little sense to many people under the age of 40 in the United States today, since American culture in many ways is diametrically opposed to many of the core values of Christianity. The various societal dynamics commonplace in American society—decrease in attachment to social groups and activities, increase in individualism and narcissistic personality traits, increased loneliness—cannot be ignored among followers of Christ. As it was in the first century after Christ, Christianity today, which at its core should be promoting *unity*, is also a countercultural movement![37]

Committed American Christians cannot ignore the culture in which they live, but they should never embrace those aspects of the culture that militate against core biblical values. They must remain "in the world, but not of it" (cf. John 17:11, 16). *In addition, Christians must also be aware that our American culture may affect the way we worship and the way we make decisions about how we should worship, decisions that may be at odds with what is central to good liturgy.* One major challenge for active Christians is to become aware of the trends in our culture that have a negative impact on the community dimensions of our faith and to examine how their own lives have been affected by such trends. We can then build upon this self-knowledge to improve how we gather together, especially around the Lord's table, in praise of our loving God.

CHAPTER 4

Worship and Prayer

The Mass, other sacramental or ritual celebrations such as baptisms or vigils for the dead, and the Liturgy of the Hours are referred to as times of "common prayer." Is this, however, the most accurate way to express what happens when Christians gather? It is true that the *General Instruction of the Liturgy of the Hours* says: "Public and common prayer by the people of God is rightly considered to be among the primary duties of the Church" (no. 1). In this case, however, the use of the term *common prayer* is amplified with the adjective *public*.

In contrast, the Constitution on the Sacred Liturgy, *Sacrosanctum Concilium* (SC), uses the term *common prayer* only to refer to the section of the Mass now called the "General Intercessions" or "Prayer of the Faithful" (see, e.g., SC nos. 53, 54). The Constitution does mention *public prayer* when referring to the Liturgy of the Hours or a shortened form of it (SC nos. 90, 98). But more often it uses the term *worship* (e.g., SC nos. 7, 33, 40) in relationship to what occurs when Christians gather.

WORSHIP IN THE CHRISTIAN EAST

Worship is a word with multiple meanings in scripture and in the Judaeo-Christian tradition. In some English translations of the Bible, "worship" is used to indicate a type of reverential obeisance toward God. For example, in Psalm 5:7, the psalmist says, "I will bow down toward your holy temple" (cf. Ps 138:2), but other translations use "worship" in place of "bow down." In such cases, *worship* has a meaning similar to *adore* and, in a sense, focuses on an attitude (and bodily posture) that a person should have before God, and on the reverence and praise that a person should render to God.

In other cases, *worship* seems to indicate a liturgical activity, performed publicly and jointly by a group of people, which is distinctly different from what is done privately and individually. This seems to be the way it is used in texts such as Psalm 95, when the psalmist says, "O come, let us worship and bow down, let us kneel before the LORD" (Ps 95:6). In these instances, *worship* focuses on the communal activity that people do together.

There is a tradition among some Eastern Christian authors that emphasizes *worship* as the *public and communal activity* done by Christians who gather at liturgy and as an activity distinctly different from *prayer*. They see prayer as something more *personal* and best done in *private*. A Web site I discovered several years ago (which, unfortunately, I have been unable to find again!) quoted an Eastern Christian bishop who said something to the effect that "if you want to pray, go home—you are here in church to worship." The good bishop was trying to stress the differences between private prayer and public liturgical worship and, to emphasize his point, used words inspired by the Sermon on the Mount ("But whenever you pray, go into your room and shut the door and pray to your Father who is in secret," Matt 6:6).

The bishop's comment, however, is not an isolated instance of a distinction between (private) prayer and (public) worship being made, especially from the Eastern Christian perspective. For example, in his book, *A Beginner's Guide to Prayer*,[1] Antiochian Orthodox Father Michael Keiser writes:

> Public worship and personal prayer are the twin support beams of the spiritual life for any believer….But they are not the same thing, and they are not interchangeable.

Worship is what we do as a group, when we gather as Christ's Body. The prayer that is offered by the Church is a united offering of prayer....

Personal prayer is just that, personal and individual. It is my own personal conversation with God, in which no one else will be involved. In personal prayer I will pray *for* others, but not *with* others....

Everyone feels the need for a little personal attention at times, and in prayer we get that; but it never replaces our worship in church. The oneness of being in the Body of Christ, united in faith and love with other believers, is both glorious and necessary. But an individual relationship with God is just as important. In order to be a complete Christian one must relate to the members of the Body of Christ together, *and* relate to God as a person. (pp. 6–7, emphasis in original)

In the *Orthodox Faith* series, in volume 2, *Worship*, Father Thomas Hopko of the Orthodox Church in America (OCA) makes the following similar comments on private, personal prayer versus public worship (called the "communal prayer of the Church") (emphasis added):

The prayers of a person *at home* differ from those *in church*, since *personal prayer* is *not the same* as the *communal prayer* of the Church. The two types of prayer are different and should *not be confused*.

When we go to church to pray, we do not go there to say our private prayers. Our private prayers should be said at home, in our room, in secret, and not in church (Matt 6:5–6)....

In church we pray with others, and we should therefore discipline ourselves to pray all together as one body in the unity of one mind, one heart and one soul. Once again this does not mean that our prayers in church should cease to be personal and unique; we must definitely put ourselves into our churchly prayer. In the Church, however, each one must put his own person with his own personal uniqueness into the common prayer of Christ with his Body....

The difficulty of many church services is that they are prayers of isolated individuals who are only physically, and not spiritually, united together.[2]

The communal dimension of public worship emphasized in Eastern Christian writings actually has roots in a biblical vision of heaven. We on earth do not gather to worship God by ourselves. Instead, we join the ongoing worship of God taking place in heaven. We experience heaven on earth through worship, and those in heaven join us as we join them in their praise of God. Isaiah 6:1–6 depicts God surrounded by seraphim who are singing "Holy, holy, holy is the LORD of hosts!" Worship is portrayed another way in Revelation 19:1–4, which narrates an early hymn depicted as the "loud voice of a great multitude in heaven." Through worship, Christians on earth unite with and "are surrounded by so great a cloud of witnesses" (Heb 12:1) who have gone before us and now worship God in heaven. This "cloud of witnesses" is "the assembly of the firstborn who are enrolled in heaven" (Heb 12:23), and the local assembly unites with them in praising our God. The liturgical texts of Eastern Christians reflect this vision. For example, during the Great Entrance in the Byzantine Eucharistic Liturgy of Saint John Chrysostom, during which the bread and wine are brought from the preparation table to the altar, the people sing:

> Let us who mystically represent the Cherubim and sing the thrice-holy hymn to the life-giving Trinity, now lay aside all earthly things so that we may welcome the King of All invisibly escorted by angelic hosts. Alleluia.

In the part of the anaphora (that is, the eucharistic prayer) that introduces the "Holy, holy, holy," the priest prays:

> We also thank you for this liturgy which you are pleased to accept from our hands, even though there stand before you thousands of archangels, tens of thousands of angels, cherubim and seraphim, six-winged, many-eyed, soaring aloft on their wings, singing, shouting, crying aloud, and saying the triumphal hymn: Holy....

These and other Eastern Christian texts continually remind those present that they are not alone in worshipping God.

WORSHIP IN THE CHRISTIAN WEST

Many Western Catholics, in contrast, have a different vision of what the Eucharistic liturgy is about. The ancient vision that those on earth join the ongoing worship of God in heaven was absent from the consciousness of most Western Catholics several generations ago. Older Western Catholics were formed in their faith practices when the Mass was still celebrated in Latin. Many younger Catholics were influenced by parents or other family members who regularly experienced the pre-Vatican II Latin Mass. In that version of the Mass, participation by the assembly in the actual liturgical texts was usually nonexistent except in a few places that had what was called a "dialogue Mass." At a dialogue Mass, the entire assembly responded to the priest in Latin with the words usually said only by the altar servers in the sanctuary. In most pre-Vatican II Masses, however, the priest spoke the Latin words of the Mass in a low voice and only the servers responded. Since very few in the church could hear the dialogue between the priest and the servers, instead of being urged to actively participate in the liturgical texts, people were encouraged to say devotional prayers such as the rosary or prayers from a prayer book during Mass, or to follow the Mass by reading a translation in a personal missal.

The official liturgical books and semiofficial catechisms did not particularly encourage any sort of involvement in the act of worship. The rubrics of the earlier, 1570 Roman Missal (often called the "Tridentine" Missal) only occasionally mentioned the presence of the people at Mass and, in fact, the rubrics describing the communion of the people during Mass seemed to be an afterthought.[3] The American Catholic *Baltimore Catechism*, which was used to teach countless Catholics the fundamentals of faith in the United States for decades before the Second Vatican Council, never mentioned the "unity" of the Body of Christ or even the presence of the assembly in its description of the Mass. When focusing on communion (e.g., question 374 in the 1953 edition), the text only describes private prayer with Christ after the reception of communion. Question 375 mentions that one effect of receiving communion is a "closer union with Our Lord," but when referring to other individuals, it says that an effect of communion is a "more fervent love...of our neighbor" without suggesting any sort of deepening union as the Body of Christ in the contemporary world.

Because of what appeared in such official publications, most Catholics saw no inconsistency between the priest celebrating Mass at the main altar while members of the congregation went to confession, said the rosary in front of statues, lit votive candles at shrines, or remained in their pew trying to follow the Mass with a people's vernacular missal. Catholics had been told that being physically present in a church while a priest was celebrating Mass was all that was needed to fulfill one's "obligation" to attend Mass on Sundays and holy days. That something more was expected of anyone present in a church was not usually in people's conscious-ness. That unity was important and that all present should be joined with others in actively participating in what was happening at the altar was rarely understood as the norm by priest or people.

Unfortunately, even though the language of the liturgy changed in 1964 and the rite of the Mass was changed in 1970, many good Catholics have never reflected on whether some com-mon practices of the early 1960s are still appropriate at Masses cel-ebrated in the early twenty-first century. In many parishes, people still sit isolated throughout the body of the church, and some may still be reciting prayers unrelated to the liturgy, while others may choose personal postures in place of the common posture used by others in the assembly.

The revered Orthodox liturgical theologian, the late Protopresbyter Alexander Schmemann, began his book, *The Eucharist: Sacrament of the Kingdom,*[4] with chapter 1 entitled "The Sacrament of the Assembly." He notes that the description of the eucharistic liturgy as the "Sacrament of the Assembly" dates to at least the fifth century (p. 12). Father Schmemann argues that any discussion of the Eucharist must begin with this fundamental real-ization. Using the typical Orthodox terminology of "temple" when referring to the physical church, he writes:

> The liturgy is the "sacrament of the assembly." Christ came to "gather into one the children of God who were scattered abroad" (John 11:52), and from the very beginning the eucharist was a manifestation and real-ization of the unity of the new people of God, gath-

ered by Christ and in Christ. We need to be thoroughly aware that we come to the temple not for individual prayer but to *assemble together as the Church*, and the visible temple itself signifies and is but an image of the temple not made by hands. Therefore, the "assembly as the Church" is in reality the first liturgical act, the foundation of the entire liturgy; and unless one understands this, one cannot understand the rest of the celebration. When I say that I am going to church, it means I am going into the assembly of the faithful in order, together with them, to *constitute the Church*, in order to be what I became on the day of my baptism—a *member*, in the fullest, absolute meaning of the term, of the body of Christ. (emphasis in original, pp. 22–23)

Elsewhere Father Schmemann bemoans the individualism that has crept into modern worship, apart from the influences of society around us.

But this "congregation of worshipers"—i.e., the assembly—has ceased to be apprehended as the primary *form* of the eucharist....Liturgical piety has become thoroughly individualistic, and the most eloquent testimony to this is the contemporary practice of receiving communion, which is completely subordinated to the "spiritual needs" of the individual believer. (p. 12)

PUBLIC WORSHIP AND PRIVATE PRAYER

To reiterate the position of the various religious writers, *worship* is fundamentally a *public and communal* activity, while *prayer* is a reality best accomplished in *private and individually*. Worship and prayer are interconnected, but are not the same. As Father Keiser writes, "The Church's worship gives a breadth of vision to our personal prayers that they would not otherwise have, keeping them from being completely centered on ourselves" (*A Beginner's Guide to Prayer*, p. 31). Understanding that *worship* differs from *prayer* is fundamental to any discussion of liturgical issues.

As an example, let us briefly reflect on gestures and postures used by the assembly during liturgy. When *praying in my room*, I can use whatever posture helps *me* pray. In fact, in *The Spiritual Exercises*, Saint Ignatius Loyola recommends that a person adopt the posture conducive for that person's prayer, and change posture as appropriate (*Spiritual Exercises*, no. 76, "4th Addition"). In contrast, when we gather for *communal worship*, *individual judgments* about participation, posture, etc., should be given less weight than to the united posture more appropriate for public gatherings, and thus for *communal public ritual activity*. Thus at Mass we should sit *together*, stand *together*, and kneel *together*, because it is *together* that we join in worship of our God.

When we come together for communal, public worship, we must always remember that, in a sense, we leave our individuality at the door and join with fellow Christians in forming the Body of Christ, thereby giving praise and worship to God. As Father Michael Keiser writes in another book, *A Beginner's Guide to Spirituality*:

> We do not gather as a collection of isolated persons who happen to encounter each other as we separately make our way toward God; we gather as members of one living organism called the Body of Christ....There is no Lone Ranger in the Christian religion, no one who is an island unto himself; the Orthodox Christian faith is the religion of a community of people.[5] (p. 27)

We all need to deepen our personal union with God. At public worship services, however, our union with God is mediated through our union with other Christians with whom we form the body of Christ in our world today. Those who complain that other people distract them from prayerful union with God (or Jesus or Mary) while at Mass (or Morning Prayer or a funeral), display a piety inconsistent with some of the foundational values of public worship. In fact, the tension between (personal) piety and (communal) liturgical worship prompted the Congregation for Divine Worship and the Discipline of the Sacraments to issue its *Directory on Popular Piety and the Liturgy* in December 2001. This *Directory* notes that "the correct relationship between Liturgy and popular piety" can "be distorted" (no. 48) and notes factors that may produce "imbalances in the relationship between the Liturgy and popular piety, to the former's detriment and the latter's impoverishment" (no. 49). Such "imbalances" may be why many people today do not seem to value the importance of forming the body of Christ, the liturgical assembly, when coming together for common worship.

In speaking to a group of French bishops in 1997, Pope John Paul II noted the importance of the assembly when he emphasized "the quality of the signs" in the liturgy. He said, "The first sign is that of the *assembly* itself…the liturgical assembly is the first image that the Church gives of herself" (March 8, 1997, no. 5).

In contrast, even contemporary Catholic writings sometimes awkwardly try to balance the *individual* aspects of being at liturgy with the *communal* aspects. For example, in his book, *The Healing Power of the Eucharist*, Father John Hampsch, CMF,[6] rightly notes the communal dimensions of the Mass when he writes:

> The fact that this Eucharistic encounter with Christ generally occurs within the context of the celebration of the Eucharist with other believers further enhances both the meaning and the power of the sacrament. The Eucharist is no longer a one-to-one encounter. It becomes the societal encounter *par excellence*, giving an

> even deeper meaning to Jesus' words in Matthew 18:20
> ["For where two or three are gathered in my name…"].
> (p. 22)

He then refers to the Hebrews 10:25, "not neglecting to meet together," and writes,

> Why does the writer admonish the believers in this
> way? Because they are missing out on that *communitar-*
> *ian* presence of Christ. It is within this communitarian
> presence that they can have the personal, sacramental
> encounter with Jesus present in the Eucharist. (p. 23)

Later, Father Hampsch notes that "true Christian community is not just a crowd of people or a juxtaposition of bodies. The group must be gathered 'in his name' in a dynamic of loving concord in order for Christ to truly dwell in that group" (p. 98). These statements rightly focus on the communal aspect of the eucharistic gathering. But someone imbued with the individualism of our contemporary culture and raised in the older Catholic piety that downplayed the importance of the assembly, may miss the impact of these communal statements. Instead, such a person may only remember another statement of Father Hampsch, namely,

> …when we spend one, two, or three minutes in fervent
> prayer right after receiving Holy Communion, our
> prayer may be more beneficial than several hours of
> fervent prayer without that sacramental presence. The
> power of the presence of Jesus gives life to our post-
> Communion prayer. (p. 82)

This focuses on a very personal, individualistic relationship between a communicant and Christ immediately after receiving communion and, unfortunately, seems to ignore the liturgical, communitarian aspects of that very same moment.

CHANGING OUR HABITS

One challenge for public, communal worship, particularly for the communal sacred meal that is the Eucharist, is to instill in people the desire to leave their personal desires, opinions, prejudices, and devotions outside of church when they come for worship. The primary desire of all present as Christians when they receive the eucharistic body of Christ should be to form the body of Christ in our world, inspired by the Spirit, and to act, move, sing, pray, give thanks, and offer supplication as one entity while they participate in worship of their God, the one Jesus called "Abba." To change the individualistic mind-set of many contemporary American Christians will not occur overnight and will need continuing education of clergy and laity alike, but if we are to fulfill the Lord's wishes, believers need to commit themselves to changing it.

Perhaps the first place to counteract individualism and encourage communal activities is the family home! Unfortunately, in contemporary American society many have daily schedules that work against the family coming together for a common meal during which they can speak to one another. Often, instead of children and parents spending evenings gathered around a single television watching the same program, family members are sequestered in different rooms watching different programs on their own televisions or playing games on personal computers. In addition, many contemporary television programs popular with children emphasize an image of an ideal American as someone who succeeds by going it alone, free of any family or community connections. Then there is the fact that smaller contemporary families mean that many children do not have the opportunity to learn how to socialize with peers within the family home.[7] Added to this is the reality that, for financial reasons, some school districts have curtailed communal, extracurricular activities, reducing additional opportunities for youngsters to learn how to socialize with peers.

A single family may not be able to turn a local school district around or change the dynamics of the local parish, but each family can reflect on how they interact together. A family in which the members rarely come together for a common meal, or watch television, play a game, or see a movie together is probably a family that is perpetuating the individualistic attitude of our contemporary world. Such families need to have "family nights" (ideally more often than once a week!), during which everyone is present, the television is off, and all engage in conversation. Perhaps families also need to discuss what television entertainment is most appropriate for younger children and does not extol individualistic (and even narcissistic) values contrary to the Christian tradition.

Similarly, a parish that does not provide opportunities for members of the parish family to come together apart from formal times for worship (social events or annual festivals), eat with each other (Lenten simple meals), study together (Bible study groups), or enjoy each other (senior citizen excursions), is a parish that may be losing opportunities to help unify parishioners in fulfillment of the Lord's prayer.

Such parishes also need to brainstorm about how the parish brings people together for more than liturgical events, however important they may be. What enables the young to know each other better, the elderly to feel acknowledged and appreciated, those active in the workforce to take time out to deepen their faith, or the sick to feel God's healing action mediated through human contact? Communities, whether civic or religious, thrive when their members reach out and make others feel a part of the whole of which they are members.

CHAPTER 5

The Unity of the Assembly through Posture and Song

There is a temptation to treat the rubrics of the Mass—especially those found in the *General Instruction of the Roman Missal* (GIRM)—as rules and recipes for right worship. Yet if one reads the GIRM solely to find *who* does *what*, *where*, and *when*, one can easily overlook the theological depth contained in the text, and especially how the GIRM weaves the biblical theme of *unity* into its understanding and explanations of practices during the eucharistic liturgy. Thus, one can easily overlook the various ways that the GIRM, especially when addressing issues of posture and song, tries to help Christians fulfill the Lord's wishes contained in John 17:21.

HERE COMES EVERYBODY

The GIRM reminds us that the Church is the "sacrament of unity" (GIRM 92), quoting from the Constitution on the Sacred Liturgy, no. 26.[1] This means that any assembly of Christians gathered for worship should reflect the unity of the Church as a whole and, in some way, itself be a "sacrament of unity" (i.e., a visible, grace-filled sign) to a much-divided world and an individualistic culture.

James Joyce, in *Finnegans Wake*, uses the wonderful phrase, "Here comes everybody," as the nickname of one of the characters, Humphrey Chimpden Earwicker, whose initials are H.C.E.

(book I, episode 2).[2] Many have used "here comes everybody" to describe an aspect of the Catholic Church: the Church in which everybody is welcome, the Church to which everybody may come. But more than being an organization whose spiritual doors are open to all, the Church is a collection of men and women, young and old, healthy and infirm, all inspired by the Holy Spirit and invited by the Lord himself to become one, as he and the Father are one. Moreover, this unity of diverse individuals becomes a visible sign, a "sacrament" for our world. It is in the context of the Church being a "sacrament of unity" that we should read and interpret references to unity in other parts of the GIRM.

Early on the GIRM cautions against any sort of divisions.

> GIRM 95: Thus, [those gathered together] are to shun any appearance of individualism or division, keeping before their eyes that they have only one Father in heaven and accordingly are all brothers and sisters to each other.

The admonition to "shun any appearance of individualism" certainly is countercultural vis-à-vis contemporary U.S. society, if we are to believe the research by Bellah, Putnam, and Twenge, mentioned earlier.

The GIRM sees unity as not only an emotional, spiritual, or mental connection with others present, but as something that is visible. Thus, we read (emphasis added):

> GIRM 96: Indeed, they form *one body*....This *unity* is beautifully apparent from the gestures and postures observed *in common* by the faithful.

Earlier the GIRM insists that personal preference should give way to visible unity through posture and gesture. Thus, we read (emphasis added):

GIRM 42: …attention should be paid to what is determined by this General Instruction and the traditional practice of the Roman Rite [regarding gestures and posture] and to what serves the *common spiritual good* of the People of God, rather than *private inclination* or arbitrary choice.

The *uniformity in posture* to be observed by all participants is a *sign of the unity* of the members of the Christian community gathered for the Sacred Liturgy.

GIRM 43: With a view to a *uniformity in gestures and postures* during one and the same celebration, the faithful should follow the directions which the deacon, lay minister, or priest gives according to whatever is indicated in the Missal.

POSTURE AS A SIGN OF UNITY

Two items are particularly noteworthy in GIRM 42. First, the GIRM sees uniformity in posture as more important than the "private inclination" of some. This goes against the cultural reverence for the individual as well as previous Catholic traditions that accepted private devotions during Mass. Second, "uniformity of posture" is fundamentally seen as a "sign of unity" rather than as primarily an act of reverence. Certainly, it is appropriate to match an appropriate posture with an action (e.g., it is appropriate to stand for the Word proclaimed in the Gospel, just as we stand when a civil dignitary enters a room). Discussion of the subject, however, often ignores the "context" given here by the GIRM, namely that a common posture is a sign of unity that all present should observe.[3]

It is noteworthy that the oldest eucharistic prayer in the current Roman Missal, the Roman Canon (Eucharistic Prayer I), uses the Latin words *omnium circumstantium* (literally, "all standing around") in the remembrance of the living to indicate those present. This indicates that at one time the people conformed to the same posture as the priest. The renowned liturgical scholar of the Roman Rite, Rev. Joseph A. Jungmann, SJ, writes that the common posture of both people and *liturgi* ("liturgists") was standing with arms outstretched.[4] In fact, there are no solid theological or liturgical reasons why there should be different postures for priest and assembly. The only time that the GIRM specifies a different posture is during the preparation of the gifts, when the presiding priest stands at the altar and the concelebrants and others in the assembly sit and join in the singing (GIRM 43). Although the Latin original of the GIRM does say that the people kneel during the consecration, it permits them to remain standing for a just cause. (The U.S. bishops have determined that in the United States, the assembly should kneel after the *Sanctus*, until the end of the Great Amen concluding the Eucharistic Prayer. In most other countries, the assembly kneels only during the institution narrative.)

There is a long tradition in the Church of seeing a common posture as a sign of *unity* as well as of *reverence*. Canon 20 of First Council of Nicaea (325) forbade kneeling on Sundays and during the Easter Season, but the canon is worded to insist on uniformity as well (emphasis added):

> Canon 20: For as much as there are certain persons who kneel on the Lord's Day and during the *Pentecoste*, therefore, to the intent that *all things may be uniformly observed everywhere*, it seems good to the holy Synod that prayer be made to God standing.[5]

A regulation from a stricter Eastern Orthodox tradition bemoans the inclusion of Western practices, but also of personal variations in posture (emphasis added):

> Orthodox Christians do not kneel *at their own pleasure*,
> but rather at the words of the priest (or deacon), "Again
> and again on bended knees…" do they kneel; the cus-
> toms of kneeling *at will* and of striking one's breast
> with the hand come from the Western heretics and are
> not permitted in the Orthodox Church. Orthodox
> Christians, in accordance with Church rule, make great
> bows *at the appointed times*, bowing to the ground and
> standing upright immediately.[6]

One should note that these norms criticize *individualism* during
common worship, not gestures per se.

In some parts of the United States, the assembly takes on various postures at the Communion Rite, between the Lord's Prayer
and the end of the Communion procession, for example, kneeling
at the "Behold the Lamb of God," and sitting or kneeling after
communion. In contrast, the original norm of the GIRM simply
states that people should remain standing until the end of Mass
(GIRM 43). (Once again, the U.S. Bishops modified the norm to
prescribe kneeling after the *Agnus Dei*, unless the diocesan bishop
determined otherwise.) The only exception permitted in the original Latin GIRM is that people may sit for the period of silence
after all have received communion and after the Communion pro-
cessional song has finished. (Again, the U.S. version of the GIRM
was modified to permit kneeling after communion.) A common
posture, once again, is a symbol of the unity of all who are participating in this act of communion.

After discussing posture, the GIRM shifts into a discussion of
other aspects of the liturgy that foster unity. It states that one purpose of the Introductory Rites is to foster unity and community
(emphasis added):

GIRM 46: [The] purpose [of the Introductory Rites] is to ensure that the faithful who come together *as one* establish *communion* and dispose themselves to listen properly to God's word and to celebrate the Eucharist worthily.

THE UNITIVE FUNCTION OF MUSIC

The GIRM also sees music and song as having a *unitive* function. We must acknowledge that many people consider music (including sung texts) to have an *aesthetical* function or a *practical* function at worship. In other words, music and singing increase the beauty of the entire worship experience (similar to beautiful architecture, stained glass windows, furniture, vesture, etc.), and they serve a practical purpose (e.g., to eliminate the silence during the preparation of the gifts). These were the qualities emphasized before the Second Vatican Council and, in themselves, they should not be downplayed. But how many people realize that music and song at worship also has a *unitive* function, at least as described in the post-Vatican II GIRM? How many people realize that this musical unity actually *serves* the liturgy and therefore has a *ministerial function* (see *Music in Catholic Worship*, no. 23; *Sing to the Lord: Music in Divine Worship*, no. 125)?

The GIRM in various places emphasizes the importance of singing at Mass, and it is in this context that we also see references to the unity of those present (emphasis added):

GIRM 39: The Christian faithful who *gather together as one* to await the Lord's coming are instructed by the Apostle Paul to sing together psalms, hymns, and spiritual songs (cf. Col 3:16).

Later, the GIRM speaks about the purpose of two key pro-cessional songs and says that one purpose is related to unity (emphasis added):

> GIRM 47: The purpose of [the Entrance] chant is to open the celebration, foster the *unity* of those who have been gathered....

> GIRM 86: [The] purpose [of the Communion chant] is to express the communicants' *union in spirit* by means of the *unity of their voices*, to show joy of heart, and to highlight more clearly the *'communitarian' nature* of the procession to receive Communion....

It is also noteworthy that the prescriptions for beginning and ending the Communion chant themselves emphasize a certain unity within the assembly.

> GIRM 86: While the priest is receiving the Sacrament, the Communion chant is begun....The singing is con-tinued for as long as the Sacrament is being adminis-tered to the faithful.

> GIRM 159: The Communion chant begins while the priest is receiving the Sacrament (cf. above, no. 86).

These directives emphasize that the Communion hymn is itself ideally a sign of unity, to be sung while *everyone*, presiding priest to last communicant, partakes of the Lord's Body and Blood. Sometime local practices may unconsciously separate the com-munion of the priest, and perhaps of other eucharistic ministers, from the communion of others in the assembly. When the priest and eucharistic ministers receive communion in silence with all in the assembly focused on them, and the Communion song does not begin until the eucharistic ministers arrive at their stations, the unintended impression is given that that the reception of communion by the ministers is somehow different from that of others in the assembly. This and similar practices are contrary to the prescriptions of the GIRM. Such practices, in fact, suggest division rather than unity.

We also should realize that, with the possible exceptions of "Happy Birthday to You," and "Auld Lang Syne" on New Year's Eve, communal singing is done less and less in the United States. For example, it is unusual to find a sporting event, or a formal school event, such as a graduation, or even a civic event, such as a presidential inauguration, in which all are invited to sing the National Anthem.[7] Communal singing events, such as a hootenanny or "Sing Along with Mitch" in the early 1960s, are few and far between. Even small-group singing moments, such as of Christmas carols by wandering carolers, or family singing, such as depicted at the beginning of "All in the Family" with Archie and Edith Bunker singing, "Those Were the Days," seem to be rare occurrences in the early twenty-first century in the United States.

As a result, in the secular sphere, Americans are less *participants* and more *spectators* when singing is involved. Where, several decades ago, communal singing had been an activity that *unified* people, physically and psychically, now singing is something a group watches someone else do *for* them. Hence, singing is yet another instance in which what we do at Mass to unite us together is countercultural, or at least goes against the grain as far as contemporary secular practices are concerned.

CHAPTER 6

Unity and the "One Bread and One Cup"

Has this happened to you? The final song has been sung at Sunday Mass, you walk out to the parking lot, and you are almost run over by someone anxious to get home to see the second half of a televised sports event. How can we eat at the same table within a church building and ignore one another outside in the parking lot? It happens, but if Christians really understood what they are doing at the Eucharist, should it ever happen? Sharing in the common loaf and the common cup should open our eyes to the presence of Christ in the community, as it did with the disciples at Emmaus. Sharing in the common loaf and the common cup should help us understand that together we form the body of Christ, and that it is our "own mystery which is placed on the Lord's table" (Saint Augustine, *Sermon* 272). Sharing in the common loaf and common cup should lead us to reach out, to bring into the unity of Christ the lost, the alienated, the rejected, the lonely, the isolated, because unity is what Christ so urgently prayed for the night before he died.

In his commentary on the Gospel of John, Saint Augustine exclaims, "O sign of unity! O bond of charity" (*In Joannis Evangelium*, 26:13) in referring to the Eucharist. The celebration of the Eucharist by Christians becomes a true sign of unity because of the very human experience of people uniting by sharing a meal. This unity is what Saint Paul expressed when he wrote, "because there is one bread, we who are many are one body, for we all partake of the one bread" (1 Cor 10:17).

ONE BREAD, BROKEN FOR ALL

In various places, the GIRM emphasizes the ideal of all present sharing in the one bread, broken at the fraction, and in the one cup, thereby forming the many present more visibly into the one body of Christ. We read the following (emphasis added):

GIRM 5: Finally, it is a people *made one* by sharing in the Communion of Christ's Body and Blood.

GIRM 72.3: Through the fraction and through Communion, the faithful, *though they are many*, receive *from the one bread the Lord's Body and from the one chalice the Lord's Blood* in the same way the Apostles received them from Christ's own hands.

GIRM 83: Christ's gesture of breaking bread at the Last Supper…signifies that *the many faithful* are made *one body* (1 Cor 10:17).

GIRM 321: The meaning of the sign demands that the material for the Eucharistic celebration truly have the appearance of food. It is therefore expedient that the Eucharistic bread, even though unleavened and baked in the traditional shape, be made in such a way that the priest at Mass with a congregation is able *in practice to break it into parts for distribution to at least some of the faithful*. Small hosts are, however, in no way ruled out when the number of those receiving Holy Communion or other pastoral needs require it. The action of the fraction or breaking of bread, which gave its name to the Eucharist in apostolic times, will bring out more clearly *the force and importance of the sign of unity of all in the one bread*, and of the sign of charity by the fact that the one bread is distributed among the brothers and sisters.

The unity of those present is much more obvious, especially with a small group, if all can partake of *one* loaf, rather than communicating from precut individual hosts. So important is this sign, that the 2004 Instruction, *Redemptionis Sacramentum*, which mostly addressed *incorrect* practices and liturgical *abuses*, emphasized that *at least part* of the bread broken at the "fraction" of the Mass should be distributed to some of those present rather than completely consumed by the celebrant.

RS 49: By reason of the sign, it is appropriate that at least some parts of the Eucharistic Bread coming from the fraction should be distributed to at least some of the faithful in Communion.

This note, though often overlooked, it is quite significant.[1] According to the rubrics of the 1570 Roman Missal in use before the reforms of the Second Vatican Council, the priest celebrant was to consume the entire "large" (about two inches in diameter) host himself. In contrast, if a priest uses such a host today, liturgical regulations urge him to consume only a portion of it and distribute other parts to those present. Ideally, one would not use a two-inch host in the contemporary Church, except when needed for exposition of the eucharistic bread in a monstrance. The liturgical regulations seem to suggest that larger hosts that can be broken into numerous pieces and distributed to those present should normally be used.

THE SIGNIFICANCE OF ONE BREAD

Some might object that food is food, so why do we need to share in *one* loaf? Perhaps a personal anecdote from a traditional American holiday may provide a concrete example. One of my most vivid memories from childhood is participating in the secular rituals associated with the family Thanksgiving Day dinner. My parents were always careful to purchase a large enough turkey to feed all invited. My mother wrapped it in cheesecloth, and my mother, sister, and I carefully made sure to baste it regularly so it would not dry out. Immediately before the dinner itself, my father would sharpen the carving knife and begin the process of carving the turkey. It would border on a secular form of "heresy" if my parents had purchased individual turkeys for each guest. Part of the tradition of Thanksgiving is that all present at the family meal share in the same turkey and thus experience their unity as a family, or through friendship, by sharing of food in common.

One additional example might also help. It is common in many restaurants to provide bread with dinner, often served in a breadbasket. Some restaurants provide individual dinner rolls for their patrons, while others provide a small loaf of bread or a baguette. I have often found the practice of having a single loaf, shared among others present at a meal, a much more familial practice. The one loaf binds people around a table together as a family by engaging each person in the action of sharing food from that common loaf.

PARTICIPATION IN THE SACRIFICE

Another aspect of eucharistic unity deals with *all present* being fed from what has been prepared for, and consecrated at, *the Eucharist being celebrated*. In this way, all fully participate in the eucharistic sacrifice[2] then taking place. Why not use what is in the tabernacle, since it is also consecrated? Although it may be practically impossible to feed several hundred people from "one loaf," and thus we accept the necessity of also using smaller hosts for the majority of communicants, it should rarely be necessary to use what is stored in the tabernacle. The consecrated bread is reserved in the tabernacle primarily for the sick and dying (see, e.g., Roman Ritual, "Holy Communion and Worship of the Eucharist outside Mass," General Introduction, no. 5 [published in 1973]). Certainly, it should *not* be the normal parish practice to *plan* to retrieve a ciborium from the tabernacle at every Mass.[3] A comparable social blunder would be to *plan* to feed some guests at Thanksgiving with food fresh from the oven, while serving others leftovers from the refrigerator. In such a case, everyone would in fact be fed, and probably no one would leave hungry. Nevertheless, there would be a significant diminishment of the unity felt by the guests when they realize that the food that should unite us in a common meal was actually prepared on separate days, for different groups.

THE MULTIPLE FACETS OF SYMBOLS

So much of religious reality and, in fact, all human reality is rooted in *symbol*. Unlike a "sign," which usually has one specific meaning (such as a "stop sign"), a symbol has multiple meanings, not all predetermined.[4] For example, a birthday or anniversary gift is rarely just the tangible object one person gives to another—it symbolizes relationships, history, and hopes. Baptism, for example, is a sign of rebirth and new life as well as of a "death" to an old way of life. Thus, the baptismal font hints at being both a womb and a tomb. Baptism is also a sign of initiation into the Church and incorporation into the Body of Christ; for this reason, in French *baptême* is the word used for any sort of "initiation." Through his research on symbols, the cultural anthropologist Victor Turner popularized the descriptions of symbols as "polysemic" (many meanings), "multivalent" (multiple appeals) and "multivocal" (multiple voices).[5] He helped people realize that in religion, as in life in general, events and objects should be interpreted more often as *symbols* rather than merely *signs*, since they often have multiple meanings. Such is the case for the Eucharist, and various authors have attempted to draw this to the attention of those who participate in this most holy meal. Monsignor Kevin Irwin focuses on some of the various aspects of the Eucharist in *Models of the Eucharist*. Not only is it a banquet (see GIRM 72), a meal that comes to us from "the table of the Lord" (GIRM 296), but it perpetuates the sacrifice[6] of the cross (GIRM 2, 11, 79d) at the altar, which is a symbol of Christ himself (GIRM 298).[7] Each Mass, a unique "sacrifice of praise and thanksgiving" (GIRM 2, *Catechism of the Catholic Church* [CCC] 1360–61), perpetuates the once-for-all sacrifice of Christ on Calvary (CCC 1364).[8] Thus, it is also appropriate to consider how the biblical understanding of "sacrifice" should influence liturgical practices.

When one also reflects on the images, given in the Hebrew Scriptures, of the people of Israel participating in *sacrifices*, one sees a presumption that all would be partaking of the animal that had been just sacrificed. Such regulations are explicit for the Passover meal (see Ex 12:8–10). They are also implicit in the description of the feast following David's sacrifice in Jerusalem when the ark was brought in (see 2 Sam 6:17–19; 1 Chr 16:1–3).

In addition, the Exodus regulations prohibit keeping any of the sacrificial lamb for the next day (Ex 12:10). A similar regulation is found regarding "the flesh of the thanksgiving sacrifice" in Leviticus (7:15). This ancient Jewish practice may have given rise to the regulation, attributed to Pope Clement I by Saint Thomas Aquinas, which prohibits reserving extra hosts for the future and orders that the clergy consume extra hosts during the Mass at which they were consecrated.[9]

FOOD FROM A SINGLE TABLE

The GIRM is very clear about the ideal of all communicants participating from what has been consecrated and demonstrating unity in this manner (emphasis added):

> GIRM 85: It is *most desirable that the faithful*, just as the priest himself is bound to do, *receive the Lord's Body from hosts consecrated at the same Mass* and that, in the instances when it is permitted, they partake of the chalice (cf. below, no. 283), so that even *by means of the signs* Communion will stand out more clearly as a participation in *the sacrifice actually being celebrated.*[10]

The first sentence is very interesting in that it explicitly states that the priest is "bound" to receive what is consecrated at the Mass,[11] and that it is "most desirable" that this rule is observed for all communicants as well. In itself, the practice expressed by this norm is yet another sign of unity, with no distinction made between layperson and priest as to the elements each receives. All receive from what has been prepared for that particular eucharistic celebration, for that particular sacrifice—no one is fed from what was consecrated earlier, at a different "sacrifice," and for the sake of a different worshipping community.

Norms for Eastern Catholic Churches are even stronger on this issue. The *Instruction for Applying the Liturgical Prescriptions of the Code of Canons of the Eastern Churches* issued by the Congregation for the Eastern Churches (January 6, 1996) states unequivocally, "The Eucharist distributed is to be that which was consecrated during the same celebration" (no. 61). In the explanatory paragraph, the *Instruction* comments:

> It is obvious that participants in a meal receive the food from the table at which they are present and not from

another. Any usage to the contrary clouds the meaning of Eucharist, which not only signifies the private communion of the individual with the Lord Jesus, but also the mutual communion in the mystical Body of Christ on the part of all the communicants, participating in the same Eucharistic Body of Christ.

This document, based on the Eastern Christian tradition, emphasizes the same truth that is found in the GIRM. Sharing in communion should be a sign of unity of all present, particularly when they receive from the *same eucharistic elements* consecrated at that eucharistic sacrifice.[12]

MASS VS. COMMUNION SERVICE

Regular use of consecrated hosts from the tabernacle also blurs the fundamental distinction between Mass and a communion service. Why prefer the Mass to a communion service? Is there any difference between merely "receiving communion" and "celebrating the Eucharist"? If the assembly always sees the tabernacle used during Mass, the important difference between the Eucharist and a communion service can be lost. The full Eucharist is a true *sacrifice* presided over by a priest with the participation of all in the assembly (see *Catechism of the Catholic Church*, no. 1365). It should include the consecration of enough bread and wine for distribution to *all present*, similar to what occurred at the sacrifices of the Old Covenant. During a priestless "communion service," the *sacrament* is, of necessity, distributed from the tabernacle, and communicants receive the eucharistic presence of Christ's Body. But those present do not participate in a "re-presentation of the sacrifice of the cross" (*Catechism of the Catholic Church*, no. 1366). Is there any difference between a person's personal reception of the *sacrament* from the tabernacle and the assembly's joining in the *sacrifice of praise* offered to God through Christ prompted by the Holy Spirit at Mass? There indeed *is* a difference! Pope John Paul II spoke, in his 2003 encyclical, *Ecclesia de Eucharistia*, of "the sacramental incompleteness of these celebrations" (no. 32). The bishops of Kansas expressed their misgivings about such services in 1995.[13] Yet how many, in fact, actually see a communion service as "incomplete"? Unfortunately, many Catholics have lost the ancient distinction between the *sacramental* and *static* aspects of the Eucharist (i.e., Christ's ongoing presence in the eucharistic elements) and the *sacrificial* and *dynamic* aspects of celebrating the Eucharist (i.e., Christ's presence in the community gathered and their recognition of the Lord "in the breaking of the bread"). Hence, because people are unaware of this ancient distinction, it is understandable why, in priestless parishes that regularly have communion services led by a deacon or layperson in place of a Mass, some people make comments such as "We prefer Sister Jane's 'Mass' because it is shorter, and we get communion just the same."[14]

When people come to understand the fundamental meaning of participating in a sacrificial meal-event and sharing the same food with fellow believers, the celebration of the Eucharist can become a radical event. How can people share a meal together and not do something for others? A sign of friendship is to invite someone over for dinner. A sign of enmity is to exclude someone from a close family gathering. When people of different backgrounds and different social status—rich and poor, healthy and feeble, women and men, people of European ancestry and people of African or Asian ancestry, CEOs and unemployed, citizen and undocumented aliens—all sit around a common table, and all share from "one bread and one cup," the very fact of eating together should put demands on everyone present. As GIRM 321 explicitly states, "sharing in the common loaf as brothers and sisters is a sign of charity of one Christian for another."

Perhaps we should also keep in the mind the Easter evening scene of the two disciples with the Risen Lord at Emmaus. It was in the action of breaking and sharing a common loaf (Luke 24:30) that the disciples recognized that the Lord was indeed risen and present with them (Luke 24:31). The message these two disciples joyously proclaimed to others after running back to Jerusalem was that they recognized the Lord "in the breaking of the bread" (Luke 24:35). How wonderful it would be for us, if our symbols were so clear and so obvious, that we can recognize that the Lord is risen and is in our midst, when we gather, and break and share the "one bread" thus uniting ourselves with one another through our participation in the Lord's own Body and Blood.

CHAPTER 7

Unity, Church Architecture, and Other Rites

Sometimes, the ideals expressed in liturgical books and documents go against the prevailing trends of our American society. We are used to eating at our own convenience, rather than at a specified time more convenient for a larger group. We prefer a special event for our own group of family and friends, rather than joining a larger community event. We do not want to wait for something, because it may disrupt our personal plans. Yet, in the face of common cultural practices, the liturgical tradition of our faith calls us to look to the common good of all followers of Christ and, indeed, of all God's children.

In the early second century, Saint Ignatius of Antioch wrote, in his *Letter to the Philadelphians*, about the importance of celebrating *one* Eucharist around *one* altar (Ignatius Phil, ch IV). The obvious consequence of a single Eucharist is that the community gathers to celebrate the Lord's Supper in common. This ideal of eucharistic unity is officially preserved in the Roman Church on Holy Thursday, where only one eucharistic celebration is permitted in any church (unless pastoral necessity demands another Eucharist) as well as on Holy Saturday, where only one Vigil is permitted. Many Orthodox churches still observe this norm, in which only one Eucharist is celebrated on any given day, or if a second Eucharist is needed, it must be celebrated on a different altar. The Code of Canon Law (can. 905) still restricts a priest to celebrating

67

only one Mass a day, unless the diocesan bishop permits priests to celebrate another Mass because of pastoral need.

The emphasis on unity and celebrating liturgical rites in common was also noted by the Constitution on the Sacred Liturgy of Vatican II, *Sacrosanctum Concilium*, which emphasized the preference for having communal celebrations of rites involving the active participation of the faithful over "a celebration that is individual and quasi-private" (SC, no. 27).

ARCHITECTURAL UNITY

The call to unity is evident in other documents or liturgical norms. At Mass, for example, the unity Christ prayed for is symbolized not only through aspects of the eucharistic celebration such as singing, posture, the use of one bread, and the use of eucharistic elements solely consecrated at that celebration. Unity is also symbolized in other ways. For example, the GIRM sees architectural elements of the worship space as contributing to unity as well. We read (emphasis added):

> GIRM 294: All these elements [of the church building], even though they must express the hierarchical structure and the diversity of ministries, should nevertheless bring about a *close and coherent unity* that is clearly expressive of the *unity of the entire holy people*.

> GIRM 303: In building new churches, it is preferable to erect a *single altar* which in the gathering of the faithful will signify the *one Christ and the one Eucharist* of the Church.

> GIRM 312: The choir should be positioned with respect to the design of each church so as to make clearly evi-

dent its character as a *part of the gathered community* of the faithful fulfilling a specific function. The location should also assist the choir to exercise its function more easily and conveniently allow each choir member full, sacramental participation in the Mass.

GIRM 318: There should usually be *only one image* of any given Saint.

GIRM 314: There should be *one* tabernacle in a church.[1]

UNIFIED CELEBRATIONS

Unity is expressed in other regulations about Masses found in the Roman Missal and elsewhere as well. For example, as noted above, the rubrics of the Roman Missal for the Holy Thursday evening Mass of the Lord's Supper state the norm that there should be a single Mass. Only if all cannot attend the single community Mass, as in large parishes that may have several Sunday Masses each weekend, may additional Masses be celebrated. (The Chrism Mass is permitted at the diocesan cathedral Holy Thursday morning, but commonly this is transferred to another day.) The Missal also forbids the celebration of more than one Easter Vigil in a parish, even if several different ethnic groups are present. The 1988 "Circular Letter Concerning the Preparation and Celebration of the Easter Feasts" issued by the Congregation for Divine Worship even encourages religious communities and other smaller communities to join for common services during the Triduum (no. 43). Elsewhere the letter also notes, "in this Vigil the faithful should come together as one..." and encourages independent, especially smaller communities, to join for a common Vigil while discouraging celebrating the Vigil "for special groups" (no. 94). Although an additional Mass can be celebrated at night *after* the

Easter Vigil if there is pastoral need, it should not be celebrated as if it were a second Vigil.

In celebrating other sacraments, the Church also prefers limiting duplications. Regarding the sacrament of baptism, the *General Introduction of Christian Initiation* (GICI) prescribes that, generally, there be a single baptism service on any given day. We read (emphasis added):

> GICI 27: As far as possible, all recently born babies should be baptized at a *common celebration* on the *same day*. Except for a good reason, baptism should *not be celebrated more than once on the same day in the same church*.

The Rite of Christian Initiation of Adults presupposes that the adult catechumens will all be initiated together, at the Easter Vigil (RCIA Introduction, no. 23). Only when there are a great number may a second ceremony be held during the Easter Octave.

Even in other rites not directly linked to the celebration of a sacrament, such as the celebration of a blessing (whether of a home, an individual, or an object such as a rosary), the norms recommend public and communal celebrations rather than individual ones. The introduction to the *Book of Blessings* notes (emphasis added):

> 16. Blessings are a part of the liturgy of the Church. Therefore their *communal celebration* is in some cases obligatory but in all cases more in accord with the character of liturgical prayer;...the presence of an assembly of the faithful is preferable.

> 17. The celebration of the blessing of things or places according to custom should not take place without the participation of at least some of the faithful.

24. For the planning of a celebration these are the foremost considerations:

> a. in most cases a communal celebration is to be preferred.... '

30. At times it may suit the occasion to have several blessings in a *single celebration*.

Even apart from those rubrics that directly pertain to the rite of the Mass, liturgical norms exhibit the pervasive nature of the Church's concern for unity. Repeatedly, Church documents show that unity is expressed and fostered in many different ways—some directly affecting the liturgical rite itself, some governing the circumstances of celebration, some addressing issues of architecture. All these references to unity remind us in many different ways that responding to Christ's prayer that *they may all be one* should be an on-going challenge to all followers of Christ.

CHAPTER 8

The Body of Christ Transforming the World

The united body of Christ that gathers in prayer at every Eucharist is not meant to stay in the physical church building, isolated from the world. Neither does the assembly cease to be the "body of Christ" when it leaves the Eucharistic celebration. The body of Christ that celebrates who it is at every Eucharist is meant to bring its talents, insights, energy, and activities, always guided by the Spirit, out into a world that needs God's presence and love so very much. The last words from the deacon or priest at Mass to those assembled are to "Go"—"Go in the peace of Christ," "Go in peace to love and serve the Lord," "*Ite, missa est,*" "Go, you are dismissed into the world." The body of Christ, nourished by the bread of life and the cup of salvation, is sent into the world at the end of each Eucharist to transform it.

"Charity begins at home," and so does *unity*. As followers of Christ, as leaven in our world (see, e.g., Luke 13:21), we cannot hope to transform our society into a more united environment without first transforming our worshipping assemblies into more Christ-like communities that show forth the "one-ness" that Christ prayed for.

SIX GOALS

In *Bowling Alone*, Putnam proposes six goals to stem the tide of growing individualism in the United States and promote what he terms *social capital*. Let me summarize those here as a prelude to discussing what Catholic communities might themselves propose to do locally. Putnam's six goals are:

> Regarding youth and schools: Increase the level of civic engagement of young adults to match that of their grandparents[1] (p. 404);
>
> Regarding the workplace: Improve the workplace so that it is more family-friendly and community-congenial (p. 406);
>
> Regarding urban design: Design communities to avoid long commutes and encourage more socializing (p. 407);
>
> Regarding religion: Spur a "great awakening" to promote a deeper engagement in a spiritual community of meaning (p. 409);
>
> Regarding arts and culture: Ensure that individuals spend less leisure time sitting passively in front of a "glowing screen" and more time in connection with people (pp. 410–11);
>
> Regarding politics and government: Ensure that more people engage in the public life of communities, including attending meetings, serving on committees, and voting (p. 412).

These six points are each worthy goals to achieve, and would go a long way to decrease the fragmentation that American society now experiences. But secular goals, however laudable, will not of themselves build up a deeper realization among Christians of the unity for which Christ prayed.[2]

Over a century ago, the prominent American minister Henry Ward Beecher (1813–87) advised seminarians at Yale to "multiply picnics" and build well equipped "church parlors"[3] (Putnam, *Bowling Alone*, p. 414). Such advice is still relevant today—church communities need reasons for parishioners to gather, aside from moments of worship, and they need neutral spaces in which to gather in smaller groups. Nevertheless, in addition to picnics and parlors, contemporary parishes also need to reflect on other things, for example, liturgical practices, home customs, and community mindset.

I acknowledge that things are more easily *said* than *done* and some things are more easily done than others. It can be straightforward to instruct musicians to begin the Communion song immediately following the "Lord, I am not worthy…" to emphasize the unity of the rite of sharing in Communion. It can also be easy to instruct sacristans always to prepare enough bread and wine to communicate all present to emphasize that we become one body by partaking in the one bread and one cup at *that* Mass. It can be easy for a parish to purchase larger hosts and tell priests they should always share part of the broken bread with the congregation.

It is more difficult, however, to change the mindset of the local community so that it sees unity as a significant value and virtue and to encourage community members to go against the current of contemporary U.S. culture. It is more difficult to convince older priests to change ritual practices they have followed for forty years or more. The individualistic mindset is quite visible, for example, when people sit scattered throughout the nave of a church, rather than gather close around the table of the Lord, or when priests give higher priority to their personal piety (or prejudices) than to liturgical ideals and principles.

It is easy to say that in Christ there is "no longer Jew nor Greek" (Gal 3:28; Col 3:11), but how do we address the challenge of a multicultural and multilingual parish? How do we avoid resorting to duplicating services during the Paschal Triduum or even duplicating celebrations of the sacrament of baptism on Sundays?

Data obtained by scholars already mentioned indicate an increase in isolation and self-focus of the younger generations and the decrease in communal activities among all generations except those born before the Second World War. If the interpretation of these data is correct, then churches in the United States cannot overlook the challenge that is before them.

Simplistic solutions will probably not have long-lasting effects, so people must reflect on the local challenges in their community. Each community needs to build on its strengths and look at various social and educational activities that it sponsors. But it must never overlook possible improvements in its liturgical life. Communities should consider modifying practices that emphasize divisions and individualism, and introducing practices that support unity and community.

NONLITURGICAL STRATEGIES

Nonliturgical parish activities also have key roles to play in fulfilling Christ's prayer for unity. Parishes cannot take on all the goals recommended by Putnam. That does not mean, however, that they should avoid doing anything.

Some parishes might begin with the youth of the parish and their religious education faculty. If the children learn in religious education classes that *unity* (or more appropriately for children, *togetherness*) is important, they can, in turn, convey that message to their families. Parishes can suggest family activities during Advent, Lent, and Easter. These can be suggested to the children in religious education classes, and such unifying activities can thus be spread to younger families in parishes.

Parishes might also brainstorm about creative ways of countering societal trends. Perhaps one parish might want to suggest that for Lent, every person give up watching television during meals, instead of giving up candy. Another parish might suggest that people forego one hour of television per day and instead attend a communal, parish-sponsored event each week such as Bible study, ongoing education with a visiting speaker, a midweek social, a "Vino and Vespers" or "Theology on Tap" session. Another parish might want to suggest that, on school nights (or at least three nights a week) families with children eat supper together and stay at table together until the last person has finished dessert! Another parish might encourage people to wear nametags during events, perhaps even at Mass. It is difficult to foster unity if you don't know the name of the person you sit next to week after week.

RETURNING TO LITURGICAL IDEALS

One should also not overlook our contemporary culture's diminished sensitivity to the impact of *symbol* in our lives and in our faith life. As noted in chapter 6, all human reality is rooted in symbol. Therefore, it is necessary to educate people about the importance of symbol in our faith and at worship, and the way symbols convey multiple meanings. The technological and scientific age in which we now live focuses on "what you see is what you get." In contrast, sacraments are fundamentally symbols in which invisible, divine grace is mediated through visible, tangible realities such as bread, wine, water, oil, touch, word. GIRM 321, speaking about the "one bread," begins by noting, *"the meaning of the sign* demands that the material for the Eucharistic celebration truly have the appearance of food" (emphasis added). Similarly, *Redemptionis Sacramentum*, 49, notes "by reason of the sign" it is appropriate to distribute some of the particles from the broken bread to communicants at that Mass. Culturally, signs and symbols do not seem as important in recent years as they once were. If Americans have no real appreciation for symbol in their day-to-day lives, the impact of symbolic gestures of unity—such as common posture, partaking of elements consecrated at that Mass—will be almost minimal. Unfortunately, too often parish leaders—priests, deacons, and pastoral ministers alike—are insensitive to the importance of symbol in liturgical rites. As a result, they cannot help those entrusted to their care to become more sensitive. For example, if priests and deacons read scriptural texts from photocopies rather than from well bound Lectionaries or Gospel books, or if they ignore the altar as the primary architectural symbol of Christ in a church and fail to reverence it properly, how can the "person in the pew" learn to appreciate the significance of symbols in Catholic liturgy? If the leaders don't realize what is important in liturgy and in Christian life, how can they lead others?

This lack of realization could be attributed partly to the fact that "old habits die hard" (to quote Mick Jagger) and that people often hesitate to participate in what is unfamiliar. Many assemblies may sing full-throated a well-known hymn such as the "Ode to Joy," but may be much more tentative singing a more recent—and unfamiliar—composition. But we also should admit that too often clergy and laity alike need to be reeducated about the ideals on which the liturgy is built. It may be helpful to recall that the 1988 "Circular Letter Concerning the Preparation and Celebration of the Easter Feasts" expressed concern that people sometimes attended *devotions* rather than the official *liturgy* during the Easter Triduum. In commenting on this reversal of priorities, the letter says (n. 3):

> Without any doubt one of the principal reasons for this state of affairs is the inadequate formation given to the clergy and the faithful regarding the paschal mystery as the center of the liturgical year and of Christian life.

UPDATING OUR FAITH

Ongoing formation is needed for all in the Church to appreciate what the Christian community is invited to experience through the liturgy, and to appreciate the role that key aspects, such as music or posture, should play in liturgical celebrations. Most professional people, whether university professors, medical doctors, or car mechanics, regularly take some time off to catch up on developments in their fields, whether through months-long sabbaticals or day-long workshops. Similarly, pastoral leaders and "people in the pew" also should regularly take time to keep up-to-date about religious issues.

It is important to come to a deeper understanding of the difference between communal acts of worship and personal prayer and piety, and to see how this affects *unity* in the contemporary Church. Understanding the foundations of worship also means becoming more sensitive to the symbolic dimension of our liturgical rites and the multitude of ways that *unity* is expressed in liturgy through symbols. Becoming sensitive is a lifelong process that will not be completed in one month or one year. But this sensitivity can begin with small changes in practices and in reflecting on documents.

In some parishes, education can be as simple as the regular inclusion in the weekly bulletin of a small excerpt about unity and liturgy taken from liturgical documents, or an excerpt about symbolism in life and in the liturgy. In other places, an occasional parish workshop offered for the benefit of lectors, Communion ministers, musicians, and others interested in liturgy, may provide the necessary stimulus for a core group of parishioners to improve their understanding of the liturgy, and their influence may be a leaven for change. No matter what a baptized Christian does during the liturgy—whether praying in the pew or presiding at the altar—it is his or her duty to participate in worship fully, actively, and consciously (as Vatican II's Constitution on the Sacred Liturgy, n. 14, reminds us). We must keep before our minds Christ's prayer for unity, and what we can do—in gesture, in song, in activities, at Mass, at home, in the workplace—to foster that unity for which he so earnestly prayed.

CHAPTER 9

Final Thoughts

We began with reflections on words of unity found in John 17:21, words that are part of a prayer that the evangelist has positioned in the context of the Last Supper. Jesus is praying to his Father, with the disciples listening, in the context of a meal at which all are gathered to partake, in common, of food and drink.

In our day, eating has devolved from a somewhat lengthy sharing of food and thoughts with family and friends to a quasi-mechanical refueling done as quickly—and with as little human interaction—as possible. Strangely, modern meals often share some of the characteristics of filling a car with gas—do it as fast as possible before the fumes get to you! So trying to address issues of unity in the context of the Eucharistic celebration is certainly countercultural.

Christianity, however, developed as a way to approach our God that was in sharp contrast to either the Jewish or Gentile cultures in which it was born. In a sense, Christianity has always been countercultural, whether the culture was Greek or Roman in the first few centuries after Christ or American at the beginning of the twenty-first century. Christians suffered persecution in the first few centuries after Christ's resurrection because they refused to buy into the prevailing culture and worship the gods of their age. When Christian missionaries moved to other parts of the world, the gospel message met new challenges and was not always accepted eagerly by indigenous peoples.

TODAY'S NEW CHALLENGES

Today, American Catholics, in particular, face new challenges. In a culture that is becoming ever more individualistic, a culture in which people do fewer and fewer communal activities, our faith in Christ still calls us to "be one." The liturgical rites we celebrate are guided by official norms that focus on unity, but unfortunately, the *unity* aspects of those norms are often overlooked. Sometimes the norms on unity go unheard because of the din of our culture extolling the virtues of the individual.

At other times, parishes ignore the norms on unity since the parish leadership, including priests, deacons, directors of religious education, and others, do not understand them because they have never assimilated them themselves. Thus, they do not even attempt to educate the local community. In other cases, the inertia of parishioners stonewalls the parish leadership.

Another significant problem is the worldwide pervasiveness of contemporary American culture. In the central section of Bangkok, Thailand, one can find a McDonald's, an Outback Steak House, and a Hard Rock Cafe. One can find similar American exports in Tokyo, Paris, or Rome. How much more U.S. "culture" will be exported—a culture that may overwhelm the ancient, and more unity-minded, cultures of other countries? Will the contemporary individualism nourished by American ways also become commonplace in most of the world, thereby damaging centuries-old values and customs that support various types of unity in those countries?

In recent discussions about contemporary cultural changes with priests from other parts of the world, there was general agreement that, with the widespread dissemination of American movies and internet access, cultural changes in the United States do affect most other nations. One person suggested it might take only five years for something popular among youth in the United States to become popular among their peers in other industrialized countries. Another person suggested that larger urban centers pick up American cultural habits more quickly than isolated rural villages, but if people in rural areas have access to the Internet, then the assimilation is quicker. Yet another noted that, in his country, young married couples are having fewer children than families a generation ago. As a result, children grow up having less social experience with peers. In single-child families, a child may grow up in an "individualistic" environment through no fault of its own, spending hours before a television or computer rather than playing with siblings or children in the neighborhood, in sharp contrast to children of an earlier generation.

SIGNS OF HOPE

There are some signs of hope, however. In some areas of the United States, recent immigrants have brought with them the kind of traditional, family-centered customs and practices that have been slowly eroding recently in much of the United States. Although some of these traditions may seem quaint when viewed through the eyes of others, especially those of European ancestry, such practices may awaken in them the desire to reevaluate how, and how often, they interact with others. In subtle ways, some of the communal aspects of recent immigrants' cultures might help counteract the individualism that pervades U.S. culture. In various places, people seem to be flocking to newly founded megachurches, a recent U.S. phenomenon. Although some may criticize megachurches on various levels, including that of theology, nevertheless their popularity suggests that many Americans still feel the desire to be a part of some sort of religious community; they will actively engage in worship and church-related activities that appeal to them.

The book is not intended to provide a litany of problems and suggested practices to solve all problems affecting American society and American Catholic parishes today. Instead it was conceived as a means to focus on John 17:21 and see how the current Roman Mass, through the GIRM, attempts to foster and to support the unity of those gathered for worship and of the greater community of which the worshippers are a part. But it also tries to raise awareness of the cultural difficulties that militate against unity becoming a reality. Hence, I have relied upon careful academic studies of contemporary American culture.

My hope, my prayer, is that the awareness of Christians may be raised regarding what the Lord desires of his flock. Christians need to assimilate Christ's prayer that "all may be one," and understand the challenges they face to make this prayer become a reality in our world. Unity must become visible in worship. It must become visible in parish outreach. It must become visible in family life. It must become visible in concern for the outcast. It must become visible in each individual. It must become visible in the gathered assembly of the faithful.

In the end, we can only do so much on our own. Ultimately, we can only join our prayers to those of the Lord, and pray, "That they may be one."

Postscript

Some readers may want to reflect a bit more on some of the issues raised in the body of this book. Some may find it helpful to reflect on these issues within a group, while others may want to reflect individually. Here are some questions to spark some thoughts.

PERSONAL:

How do I see myself in relation to other men and women? Do I see myself as "one" with other men and women, sharing some of the same strengths and weaknesses of family, friends, acquaintances, neighbors, and coworkers?

How engaged am I with my local community, parish, co-workers?

Do I ever invite my coworkers to my home for dinner or a party? Do I ever interact with my colleagues in non-job-related settings?

Do I belong to any community (or work-related) sports teams (softball, bowling league)?

Do I belong to any organizations, such as the Elks, Rotary Club, Knights of Columbus, or Women's Club?

Do I meet regularly with others as part of a card-playing club, book discussion group, Bible study group, faith-sharing group?

What other types of activities could I get involved in to help me become more a part of my local community and more connected with my coworkers or neighbors?

How do I see myself in relation to the American culture? Am I drawn toward the "individualism" aspects or the "equality" aspects of U.S. culture?

FAMILIAL:

How often does my whole family eat dinner together? Is the ambience of dinner at home any different than it would be if each ate individually at a fast food restaurant?

Is dinner a time for conversation or for watching television?

Are the television programs watched, especially by younger children, more reflective of exaggerated individualism and narcissism than of the fundamental social nature of society and of the Christian community?

How often does my family engage in communal activities such as a movie, church, a sports event, dinner at a restaurant, a Sunday afternoon walk or drive, or a parlor game?

How often do I connect with extended family (cousins, aunts/uncles, nephews/nieces) in my area?

What other type of activities could be done in my home to foster more connectedness within my immediate family and with my extended family?

CHURCH:

Does my parish sponsor nonliturgical activities that bring people together such as Lenten fish fries or "soup and substance" meals, annual fiestas, "Theology on Tap," guest speakers, annual parish missions, or days of recollection?

Do people actively participate *as a body* during Mass or does the assembly seem to be a group of people who are unaware of others in their posture or seating locations?

Do parishioners know each other's names, and are they welcoming to strangers? Should parishioners occasionally (or regularly) wear nametags to help such interactions take place?

Does the parish sponsor activities to bring various constituencies together, such as teens, senior citizens, young adults, and the widowed? Are there service activities for high school students, excursions for retired persons, support groups for those with special needs?

Do I participate in my parish as a liturgical minister (lector, Communion minister, usher, choir member) or in another way? Could I get involved in something as simple as occasionally visiting the homebound or telephoning someone?

What type of outreach is there in my parish (e.g., to non-Catholics, to the poor)? Have I contributed in any way to such outreach?

What other types of activities can bring more people together and create more "social capital" in my local parish?

COMMUNITY:

Are there civic social activities that need to be fostered?

Does my city provide special assistance to enable senior citizens or the disabled to socialize, such as special transportation? Does it have senior centers with special social programs?

Does my city provide sports and social activities for teenagers?

What other types of supports/infrastructures for socializing are needed in my community? Have I raised these concerns with city government?

Notes

Bibliographical references to books in the following notes are given (after the first reference) in abbreviated form, by author and book title only.

CHAPTER 2

1. Literally, the text uses the word for "recline at table." "Reclining at table" was the posture for a festive meal rather than an ordinary meal. See Joachim Jeremias, *The Eucharistic Words of Jesus* (London: SCM Press, 1966), 48ff.

2. Joachim Jeremias, *New Testament Theology: The Proclamation of Jesus* (New York: Charles Scribner's Sons, 1971), 115f.

3. The difference between the eucharistic bread and wine and ordinary food was also emphasized a century later by Saint Justin Martyr in his *First Apology*, when he noted "We do not consume the [Eucharistic bread and wine] as ordinary food and drink, for we have been taught that...the food our flesh and blood assimilates has become the flesh and blood of the incarnate Jesus by the power of his own words contained in the prayer of thanksgiving" (chap. 66).

4. For a brief discussion about the radical egalitarian nature of the Christian Eucharist, see, for example, Charles A. Bobertz, "Holy Week and the Triduum," *Rite*, 38:1 (Jan/Feb 2007): 5–7, especially p. 6, where the author comments on the readings of Holy Week and the Triduum. Bobertz describes early Christian

Eucharists in this way: "It was, literally, the enactment of a human community restored to a right relationship with God and with each other, a bold vision of a restored Genesis creation." The Eucharist, at which Jews and Greeks, slave and freemen, women and men, all ate together, is a symbol of the world before the divisions precipitated by the fall of Adam and Eve, just as Pentecost reverses the divisions of languages attributed to the Tower of Babel.

5. The liturgical texts in the Roman Missal contain numerous other references to unity. For example, the Preface for Sundays in Ordinary Time VIII says, "You gather [your children] into your Church, to be one as you, Father, are one with your Son and the Holy Spirit." The Eucharistic Prayers for Masses for Various Needs and Occasions mention unity in various ways. Version I includes the words, "Strengthen the bonds of unity between the faithful and their pastors, that...your people may stand forth...as a sign of oneness and peace." Version II reads, "Strengthen in unity those you have called to this table" and version III prays, "Strengthen the bonds of our communion with N. our pope...and all your holy people." The Prayer after Communion for the Fifth Sunday in Ordinary Time says, "God our Father, you give us a share in the one bread and the one cup and make us one in Christ."

CHAPTER 3

1. Alexis de Tocqueville, *De la démocratie en Amérique*. 2 vols. (Paris: Librairie de Charles Gosselin, 1835–40). Various translations and editions have been published in English. For example, *Democracy in America*, trans. Arthur Goldhammer (New York: Library of America, 2004).

2. See Robert D. Putnam, *Bowling Alone: The Collapse and Revival of American Community* (New York: Simon & Schuster, 2000), 24. Tocqueville, *Democracy in America*, trans. Goldhammer, vol. 2, 585.

3. U.S. Declaration of Independence, par. 2.

4. Putnam, *Bowling Alone*, 48. Tocqueville, *Democracy in America*, trans. Goldhammer, vol. 2, 595.

5. See Jean M. Twenge and W. Keith Campbell, *The Narcissism Epidemic: Living in the Age of Entitlement* (New York: Free Press, 2009), 57–58. The authors note that the "recipe for American individualism" combined "individual freedom tempered with equality." They also note that the contemporary emphasis on how "special" individuals are (e.g., 16, 192) eclipses an underlying notion of "equality" and the realization that there can be more that unites individuals together than separates them.

6. Robert N. Bellah et al., *Habits of the Heart: Individualism and Commitment in American Life* (Berkeley: University of California Press, 1987).

7. Kevin W. Irwin, in *Models of the Eucharist* (New York: Paulist Press, 2005), comments that the communal celebration of the Eucharist itself can be seen to be countercultural, given that Americans value individual freedoms so highly (71).

8. Contemporary U.S. culture presents one set of challenges to religious practices. Other cultures may present other types of challenges. A *New York Times* article published July 16, 2007, entitled "Japan Learns Dread Task of Jury Duty," by Norimitsu Onishi, described the difficulties Japan was facing in training its citizens how to serve on juries. The author comments, "But for [the jury system] to work, the Japanese must first overcome some deep-rooted cultural obstacles: a reluctance to express opinions in public, to argue with one another and to question authority."

9. In 1988, Father Francis Mannion authored a well-documented scholarly paper on the interplay of contemporary culture and liturgy. See M. Francis Mannion, "Liturgy and the Present Crisis of Culture," *Worship* 62:2 (March 1988): 98–123. In it, he mentions the problems of individualism and a decrease in social connections.

10. Martin F. Connell, "On the U.S. Aversion to Ritual Behavior and the Vocation of the Liturgical Theologian," *Worship* 78:5 (September 2004): 386–404.

11. A Google search of "epidemic loneliness" in June 2009 produced a listing of about 238,000 pages.

12. Putnam, *Bowling Alone*.

13. Robert Wuthnow, *The Restructuring of American Religions: Society and Faith Since World War II* (Princeton: Princeton University Press, 1988).

14. Putnam, *Bowling Alone*, 18–19. "Whereas physical capital refers to physical objects and human capital refers to properties of individuals, social capital refers to connections among individuals—social networks and the norms of reciprocity and trustworthiness that arise from them."

15. Ibid., 20.

16. Even nonspectator, nonorganized sports that usually are not played alone, such as golf and tennis, are falling on hard times. This phenomenon was noted in a column in the *New York Times* by Paul Vitello (February 21, 2008) entitled, "More Americans Are Giving Up Golf."

17. Although not cited by Putnam, Gallup statistics cited by CARA (The Center for Applied Research in the Apostolate) indicate that weekly Mass attendance in the United States declined from a peak of about 74 percent in 1958 to about 40 percent in 2003. CARA statistics from September 2000 to September 2004 indicated weekly Mass attendance to be between 31 percent and 39 percent. See January 10, 2005, report from The Center for Applied Research in the Apostolate (CARA), Georgetown University, http://cara.georgetown.edu/AttendPR.pdf.

18. This is a fact that may have significant consequences for celebrating the Eucharistic meal together "as a family." See also comments by Irwin, *Models of the Eucharist*, 50–51. Irwin refers to a 1993 academic paper by Margaret Mackenzie entitled, "Is the

Family Meal Disappearing?" in *The Journal of Gastronomy* 7:1 (Winter/Spring 1993): 34–45.

19. Jean M. Twenge, PhD, *Generation Me: Why Today's Young Americans Are More Confident, Assertive, Entitled—and More Miserable Than Ever Before* (New York: Free Press, 2006).

20. On individualism, also see Putnam, *Bowling Alone*, 24.

21. Peter J. Pestillo, "Can the Unions Meet the Needs of a 'New' Work Force?" *Monthly Labor Review* 102 (February 1979): 33. Quoted in Putnam, *Bowling Alone*, 82.

22. Thomas E. Patterson, *Doing Well and Doing Good: How Soft News and Critical Journalism Are Shrinking the News Audience and Weakening Democracy—And What News Outlets Can Do About It* (Cambridge, MA: Harvard Kennedy School Joan Shorenstein Center on the Press, Politics, and Public Policy), 5. PDF available at http://www.hks.harvard.edu/presspol/publications/reports/soft_news_and_critical_journalism_2000.pdf (accessed November 6, 2009).

23. See Twenge and Campbell, *The Narcissism Epidemic*. "In one dataset, Americans scored in the top 10–20 percent of nations on narcissism. In another study, Americans obtained higher narcissism scores than people from any other country" (37).

24. Ibid. The authors contrasted a study of Korean advertisements that focused on being like others (185) and notes the collectivistic attitudes of Scandinavians (263). See Heejung Kim and Hazel R Markus, "Deviance or uniqueness, harmony or conformity? A cultural analysis," *Journal of Personality and Social Psychology* 77 (1999): 785–800.

25. Jeffrey J. Arnett, *Emerging Adulthood: The Winding Road from the Late Teens through the Twenties* (New York: Oxford University Press, 2004).

26. A Google search of "spiritual versus religious" in June 2009 produced a listing of over 84 million pages.

27. Twenge's evaluation of the data, particularly as indicative of greater "narcissism," is not without critics, however. Professors Kali Trzesniewski, Brent Donnellan, and Richard Robins, in "Do Today's Young People Really Think They Are So Extraordinary? An Examination of Secular Trends in Narcissism and Self-Enhancement" (*Psychological Science* 19:2 [Feb 2008]: 181–88) provide data that seem to rebut Twenge's conclusions. The difference in conclusions among academic scholars, on the other hand, does not negate the raw scientific data gathered by scholars such as Putnam and others, and those data do indicate less involvement in communal activities.

28. Dorothy Day, *The Long Loneliness: The Autobiography of Dorothy Day* (New York: Curtis Books, 1952), 315–16.

29. Robert Wuthnow, *After the Baby Boomers: How Twenty- and Thirty-Somethings Are Shaping the Future of American Religion* (Princeton: Princeton University Press, 2007). See Wuthnow's chapter 4 for comments on different religious denominations and his chapter 9 for comments on Hispanic Catholics.

30. David Brooks, "The Power of Marriage," Opinion, *New York Times*, November 22, 2003.

31. John Leland, "It's My Funeral and I'll Serve Ice Cream if I Want To," *New York Times*, July 20, 2006.

32. Thomas Lynch, "Our Near-Death Experience," Opinion, *New York Times*, April 9, 2005. Lynch comments on the funeral of Pope John Paul II and notes the stark contrast to many contemporary funerals where "the 'celebration of life' involves a guest list open to everyone except the actual corpse." At the papal funeral, the body of the deceased and widely-beloved pontiff was a unifying focal point for traditional funeral rites that brought mourners together (many via television) and enabled them to sing together, pray together, shed tears together, and bid farewell together to someone they had known for over twenty-five years. Both the presence of the body and the familiar ritual provided a cohesive unity

to the papal rites that contrasted with the experience of many people who attend contemporary "memorial services."

33. See Twenge and Campbell, 188. The authors note that individual cell phones mean that less interaction may take place within a family since "teenage siblings no longer have to fight over the phone line."

34. At a Broadway musical I attended in July 2007, an audience member in the row behind me thought nothing of answering her cell phone during the performance and trying to whisper, "I'm sorry, I can't talk to you right now."

35. The complete report is available at http://religions. pewforum.org/pdf/report-religious-landscape-study-full.pdf (accessed November 6, 2009).

36. See page 3 of the Winter 2008 CARA report, "The Impact of Religious Switching and Secularization on the Estimated Size of the U.S. Adult Catholic Population," accessible at http://cara. georgetown.edu/Winter%202008.pdf (accessed November 6, 2009).

37. To put things into a broader context, the United States is not the only nation in which Christianity is countercultural. I was moved when I read about the Thai Christian artist Sawai Chinnawong at a showing of some of his paintings in the Museum of Biblical Art of the American Bible Society in New York City. He commented that, because he came from a predominantly Buddhist culture and because Buddha is never depicted as suffering in Buddhist iconography, it was difficult for him to portray the "suffering of Christ, which is the hardest spiritual concept for us to understand or accept." As Christianity is countercultural in the United States, it may also be countercultural, albeit in different ways, in other parts of the world as well.

CHAPTER 4

1. Michael Keiser, *A Beginner's Guide to Prayer: The Orthodox Way to Draw Closer to God* (Ben Lomond, CA: Conciliar Press, 2003).

2. Father Thomas Hopko, *Worship*, vol. 2 of *The Orthodox Faith* (New York: Department of Religious Education, The Orthodox Church in America, 1972), 61–62. The text is also available at: http://www.oca.org/OCchapter.asp?SID=2&ID=60 (accessed November 6, 2009).

3. 1570 *Missale Romanum, Ritus Servandus in Celebratione Missæ*, X. After describing in no. 5 the communion of the priest, the purification of the vessels, and the covering of the chalice, no. 6 begins with the words, *"Si qui sunt communicandi in Missa, Sacerdos post sumptionem Sanginis, antequam se purificet...* (If there are any to be communicated during Mass, the priest after drinking the Blood, before he purifies himself...)"* and then describes the procedure to be followed when anyone receives communion during Mass. The presumption of the rubrics was that people did not receive communion during Mass and, in fact, the corresponding Roman *Pontifical*, the book containing the liturgical ceremonies for bishops, forbade the reception of communion by anyone other than the bishop at the Chrism Mass on Holy Thursday morning!

4. Alexander Schmemann, *The Eucharist: Sacrament of the Kingdom* (Crestwood, NY: St. Vladimir's Seminary Press, 1988).

5. Michael Keiser, *A Beginner's Guide to Spirituality: The Orthodox Path to a Deeper Relationship with God* (Ben Lomond, CA: Conciliar Press Ministries, 2007).

6. John H. Hampsch, CMF, *The Healing Power of the Eucharist* (Cincinnati: Servant Books, 1999).

7. One cannot deny that families are smaller than they had been a few decades ago (see, e.g., "The Rise of the Only Child," *Newsweek*, April 23, 2001), and the reasons given are many, such as working mothers, delayed childbearing, economic constraints.

According to the *Newsweek* article, the French sociologist Jean-Claude Kaufman relates the rise in one-child families to "the growth of individualism." Although all the ramifications of (and reasons for) smaller families may still be tentative, one cannot ignore the reality and wonder how this affects religious ideals.

CHAPTER 5

1. The Council document itself references Saint Cyprian, *On the Unity of the Catholic Church*, 7. This paragraph of the Constitution on the Sacred Liturgy is repeated almost verbatim as the first part of canon 837 of the *Code of Canon Law* and in no. 1140 of the *Catechism of the Catholic Church*.

2. James Joyce, *Finnegans Wake* (New York: Viking Press, 1947), 30–32.

3. Canon 17 of the *Code of Canon Law* states a general canonical norm: "Ecclesiastical laws must be understood in accord with the proper meaning of the words considered in their *text* and *context*…" (emphasis added). Any discussion of the *text* of liturgical norms (i.e., the actual determination of when the assembly stands, sits, or kneels) must first acknowledge the *context* for any posture, which is, according to the GIRM, that posture is "a sign of unity."

Thus, in situations where a significant number of those in the assembly would have to assume a different posture (e.g., some kneeling and others standing), it seems to be more in keeping with the intent of GIRM 42 that all stand. For example, at a "standing-room only" Easter Sunday or Christmas Day Mass, one would be justified in asking everyone to remain standing during the Eucharistic Prayer since the "sign of unity" via a common posture would be more important (according to the spirit of the GIRM) than to have some people observing the U.S. practice of kneeling during part of the Eucharistic Prayer while others have to stand.

Also, because a difference of posture seems not to be a "sign of unity," some dioceses (e.g., Los Angeles) have determined that, in keeping with the spirit and letter of the GIRM, everyone is to remain standing (and singing) throughout the Communion Rite until *all sit down together* after the last communicant has received the Eucharist and the celebrant returns to his chair and sits. Upon reflection, it does seem odd that the only time at Mass in many churches that the assembly displays significant "disunity" in posture (with some people standing, others sitting, others kneeling) is during "communion," when everyone should be united to Christ and to one another as the body of Christ! For example, see Cardinal Roger Mahony's 1997 Pastoral Letter, *Gather Faithfully Together*, written for the Archdiocese of Los Angeles. (Available as: Roger Cardinal Mahony, *Gather Faithfully Together: Guide for Sunday Mass* [Chicago: Liturgy Training Publications, 1997].) In the section entitled, "The Liturgy of the Eucharist," we read (no. 73): "This Sunday's single Communion song continues until presider and assembly sit down after all have taken Holy Communion." This practice was reiterated in Cardinal Mahony's letter, "Deepening the Spirit of Renewal," of October 24, 2003, published in *The Tidings*, the newspaper of the Archdiocese of Los Angeles.

4. See Joseph A. Jungmann, SJ, *The Mass of the Roman Rite: Its Origins and Development (Missarum Sollemnia)*, trans. Francis A. Brunner, CSSR (1959; repr. Westminster, MD: Christian Classics, 1974), 172, 246–47.

5. Earlier, Tertullian (second–third centuries) forbade fasting and kneeling on Sundays since it was a sign of penance, considered incompatible with the joy that should be shown by all on Sundays. "We consider it unlawful to fast, or to pray kneeling, upon the Lord's day; we enjoy the same liberty from Easter day to that of Pentecost" (Tertullian, *De corona militis*, 3, 4).

6. *Orthodox Life*, 26:1 (Jan–Feb, 1976), 24–27. Also available online at: http://freepages.genealogy.rootsweb.ancestry.com/~pocky/gnisios/howchurch.html (accessed November 6, 2009).

7. Probably more people could write out the text of the Nicene Creed correctly than the text of the U.S. national anthem at this point in U.S. history.

CHAPTER 6

1. Also see *Introduction to the Order of Mass*, (USCCB, Bishops' Committee on the Liturgy, 2003), no. 130, bullet 3.

2. The use of *sacrifice* in reference to the Mass is long-standing and is found, for example, in the writings of St. Augustine (350–430), *De civitate Dei*, bk. 10, chap. 6.

3. Even though the GIRM mentions that the excess consecrated bread may be put in the tabernacle after the distribution of communion (GIRM 163), nowhere does it mention that previously consecrated hosts in the tabernacle may be distributed at Mass. In fact, GIRM 85 and previous documents from the Holy See all insist that those present should receive communion from what had been consecrated at that same Mass. See, e.g., Dennis C. Smolarski, SJ, *How Not to Say Mass* (revised ed.) (New York: Paulist Press, 2003), 74–75.

One should note the special concern of Pope Benedict XIV (pope 1740–1758). In his apostolic letter, *Certiores effecti* (Nov 13, 1742), he encouraged the distribution of elements consecrated *at that Mass* during the communion of the faithful and to avoid distributing what was in the tabernacle. As Monsignor Irwin writes:

> [A]s early as the pontificate of Pope Benedict XIV, taking hosts from the tabernacle was regarded as an abnormality for theological reasons....The difficulty that Benedict XIV perceived was that the faithful would

come to understand that the sacrament of the
Eucharist was available in the tabernacle and that the
Eucharistic sacrifice was experienced (only) at Mass.
For him, the liturgical practice of distributing communion from the tabernacle could easily cause confusion because it separated sacrifice from presence....He
judged that [the practice of communicating the faithful
from hosts consecrated at that Mass] would help to
underscore the integrity of Eucharistic theology.
(Irwin, *Models of the Eucharist*, 181–82)

4. See, for example, Raymond Firth, *Symbols: Public and Private* (Ithaca, NY: Cornell University Press, 1973), 74–75.

5. See, for example, Mari Womack, *Symbols and Meaning: A Concise Introduction* (Plymouth: Roman Altamira, 2005), 3.

6. The 1967 Instruction *Eucharisticum mysterium*, notes that the Mass "is at once and inseparably" a sacrifice perpetuating the sacrifice of the cross, a memorial of Christ's death and resurrection, and a sacred banquet (no. 3). In his 2004 Apostolic Letter, *Mane nobiscum*, Pope John Paul II noted the "meal," "memorial," and "sacrificial" aspects of the Eucharist in the same paragraph (no. 15).

7. Also see Preface for Easter V where Christ is said "to be the priest, the altar, and the lamb of sacrifice."

8. Detailed contemporary scholarly summaries on the theology of sacrifice can be found in Edward J. Kilmartin, SJ, *The Eucharist in the West: History and Theology* (Collegeville, MN: Liturgical Press, 1998), especially part two (241 ff.), which focuses on eucharistic sacrifice. A more recent book is Robert J. Daly, SJ, *Sacrifice Unveiled: The True Meaning of Christian Sacrifice* (London / New York: Continuum, 2009). Daly edited Kilmartin's book and continues the historical and theological development of his thought.

9. Saint Thomas Aquinas, *Summa Theologica*, IIIa, q 83, art 5, ad 1. "Hence, as is laid down (*De Consecr.*, dist. ii), Pope Clement I ordered that 'as many hosts are to be offered on the altar as shall suffice for the people; should any be left over, they are not to be reserved until the morrow, but let the clergy carefully consume them with fear and trembling.' "

10. Footnote 73 in the GIRM. Cf. Sacred Congregation of Rites, Instruction *Eucharisticum mysterium* (On the Worship of the Eucharist), 25 May 1967, nos. 31, 32; Sacred Congregation for the Discipline of the Sacraments, Instruction *Immensae caritatis*, 29 January 1973, no. 2: AAS 65 (1973), 267–68.

11. See the discussion in Saint Thomas Aquinas, *Summa Theologica*, IIIa, q. 82, art. 4; Pius XII, Encyclical *Mediator Dei*, nos. 112, 115. The regulations presupposing that the priest will eat from the bread and wine he has consecrated at Mass is reminiscent of the regulations found in Leviticus 7:5–6, which describes the "guilt offering" and the priests partaking of the oblation they just made.

12. Among the various realities associated with the eucharistic celebration, perhaps three have been key in the consciousness of most Catholics: (1) (real/sacramental) presence (i.e., of Christ's Body and Blood under the species of bread and wine), (2) sacrifice (perpetuating Christ's sacrifice on Calvary), and (3) meal (commemorating the Last Supper). Irwin, in *Models of the Eucharist*, goes into depth about these three and other images associated with the Eucharist. It seems, however, that the past, almost exclusive, emphasis on (real) presence by many Catholics has resulted in a static and individualistic focus on the eucharistic elements in the tabernacle, rather than an appreciation for the dynamic and communal liturgical implications of participating in a banquet (meal) or a biblical sacrifice (of praise). This almost exclusive past emphasis on "presence" may be one reason why it is so difficult to change the all-too-common practice of using what is in the tabernacle during Mass. If one ignores the "meal" and "sacrifice" aspects of a

eucharistic celebration and only focuses on "presence," one could (erroneously) conclude that there is nothing improper with using what is in the tabernacle during Mass.

13. Pastoral Message of the Bishops of Kansas on Sunday Communion without Mass, "Sunday Eucharist—Do This in Memory of Me," June 18, 1995. Also see comments in Irwin, *Models of the Eucharist*, 10–12, 140–41.

14. See the discussion of this topic in Thomas Richstatter, OFM, "Mass and Communion Service: What's the Difference?" published in 1999 as one of the *Catholic Update* series by the St. Anthony Messenger Press. Available on line at http://www.americancatholic.org/Newsletters/CU/ac0999.asp (accessed November 6, 2009).

CHAPTER 7

1. This norm about a single tabernacle is actually a restatement of an earlier norm published in the 1967 "Instruction on the Eucharistic Mystery." There we read (no. 52), "Therefore, as a rule, each church should have only one tabernacle."

CHAPTER 8

1. Putnam's data show how significant "social capital" (of parents) can be for the education of their offspring (see *Bowling Alone*, 299–306). Putnam questions the practice of schools (and parents) focusing on the tangible rather than examining intangible human "connections." He writes:

> [W]hat this admittedly crude evidence is saying is that there is something about communities where people connect with one another—over and above how rich or poor they are materially, how well educated the adults

themselves are, what race or religion they are—that positively affects the education of children. Conversely, even communities with many material and cultural advantages do a poor job of educating their kids if the adults in those communities don't connect with one another.... (301)

Parents in states with high levels of social capital are more engaged with their kids' education, and students in states with high levels of social capital are more likely than students in less civic states to hit the books rather than to hit one another (302)

[Anthony S.] Bryk and his colleagues [authors of large, multiyear studies of Chicago schools and of Catholic schools nationwide] conclude that Catholic schools do better than public schools not because the teachers or students are more qualified, but because "Catholic schools benefit from a network of social relations, characterized by trust, that constitute a form of 'social capital.'" (304)

2. Twenge and Campbell, in chapter 17 of *The Narcissism Epidemic*, propose their own list to stem the "epidemic." These include personal changes, such as "quieting the ego," and emphasizing similarities with others; cultural changes, such as de-emphasizing self-admiration; and changes in social practices, such as in parenting, education, the media, the internet, and in economic policies (see 280–303).

3. Henry Ward Beecher, *Lecturers on Preaching*, Second Series (London: T. Nelson and Sons, 1874), 177–78.

Bibliography

Arnett, Jeffrey J. *Emerging Adulthood: The Winding Road from the Late Teens through the Twenties*. New York: Oxford University Press, 2004.

Beecher, Henry Ward. *Lectures on Preaching*. Second Series. London: T. Nelson and Sons, 1874.

Bellah, Robert N., et al. *Habits of the Heart: Individualism and Commitment in American Life*. Berkeley: University of California Press, 1987.

Connell, Martin F. "On the U.S. Aversion to Ritual Behavior and the Vocation of the Liturgical Theologian." *Worship* 78, no. 5 (September 2004): 386–404.

Daly, Robert J., SJ. *Sacrifice Unveiled: The True Meaning of Christian Sacrifice*. London/NewYork: Continuum, 2009.

Day, Dorothy. *The Long Loneliness: The Autobiography of Dorothy Day*. New York: Curtis Books, 1952.

Hampsch, John H., CMF. *The Healing Power of the Eucharist*. Cincinnati: Servant Books, 1999.

Irwin, Kevin W. *Models of the Eucharist*. New York: Paulist Press, 2005.

Joyce, James. *Finnegans Wake*. New York: Viking Press, 1947.

Jungmann, Joseph A., SJ. *The Mass of the Roman Rite: Its Origins and Development (Missarum Sollemnia)*. Translated by Francis A. Brunner, CSSR. New York: Benziger Brothers, 1959. Reprint, Christian Classics, Westminster, MD, 1974.

Keiser, Michael. *A Beginner's Guide to Prayer: The Orthodox Way to Draw Closer to God.* Ben Lomond, CA: Conciliar Press, 2003.

Keiser, Michael. *A Beginner's Guide to Spirituality: The Orthodox Path to a Deeper Relationship with God.* Ben Lomond, CA: Conciliar Press Ministries, 2007.

Kilmartin, Edward J., SJ. *The Eucharist in the West: History and Theology.* Edited by Robert J. Daly, SJ. Collegeville, MN: Liturgical Press, 1998.

Kim, Heejung, and Markus, Hazel R. "Deviance or uniqueness, harmony or conformity? A Cultural Analysis." *Journal of Personality and Social Psychology.* 77 (1999): 785–800.

Mahony, Roger Cardinal. *Gather Faithfully Together: Guide for Sunday Mass.* Chicago: Liturgy Training Publications, 1997.

Mannion, M. Francis. "Liturgy and the Present Crisis of Culture." *Worship* 62, no. 2 (March 1988): 98–123.

Pestillo, Peter J. "Can the Unions Meet the Needs of a 'New' Work Force?" *Monthly Labor Review* 102 (February 1979).

Putnam, Robert D. *Bowling Alone: The Collapse and Revival of American Community.* New York: Simon & Schuster, 2006.

Schmemann, Alexander. *The Eucharist: Sacrament of the Kingdom.* Crestwood, NY: St. Vladimir's Seminary Press, 1988.

Smolarski, Dennis C., SJ. *How Not to Say Mass: A Guidebook on Liturgical Principles and the Roman Missal.* Rev. ed. New York: Paulist Press, 2003.

Tocqueville, Alexis de. *De la démocratie en Amérique*, Paris: Librairie de Charle Gosselin, 1835–1840. Translated by Arthur Goldhammer as *Democracy in America.* New York: Library of America, 2004.

Twenge, Jean M., PhD. *Generation Me: Why Today's Young Americans Are More Confident, Assertive, Entitled—and More Miserable Than Ever Before.* New York: Free Press, 2006.

Twenge, Jean M., Ph.D., and W. Keith Campbell, PhD. *The Narcissism Epidemic: Living in the Age of Entitlement*. New York: Free Press, 2009.

Wolfe, Tom. "The 'Me' Decade and the Third Great Awakening." *New York*, August 23, 1976.

Wuthnow, Robert. *The Restructuring of American Religions: Society and Faith since World War II*. Princeton: Princeton University Press, 1988.

———. *After the Baby Boomers: How Twenty- and Thirty-Somethings Are Shaping the Future of American Religion*. Princeton: Princeton University Press, 2007.